PEACING TOGETHER

By the same author:

SECONDS AWAY!
TEAM SPIRIT

PEACING TOGETHER

From conflict to reconciliation

DR DAVID CORMACK

MARC
Eastbourne

Biblical quotations are from the
New International Version
© International Bible Society 1973, 1978, 1984
Published by Hodder and Stoughton

Cover design by Drummond and Peggy Chapman

British Library Cataloguing in Publication Data

Cormack, David
    Peacing together.
    1. Interpersonal relationships. Conflict.
    Settlement. Role of mediation.
    I. Title
    303.6

    ISBN 1-85424-085-4 (MARC)
        0-86760-075-6 (Albatross)

Co-published in Australia by
Albatross Books, PO Box 320, Sutherland, NSW 2232

Printed in Great Britain for
MARC, an imprint of Monarch Publications Ltd
1 St Anne's Road, Eastbourne, East Sussex BN21 3UN by
Richard Clay Ltd, Bungay, Suffolk.
Typeset by Nuprint Ltd, Harpenden, Herts AL5 4SE

To
the pilots and staff of
Mission Aviation Fellowship
whose vision puts them
in the front line of the battle

INTRODUCTION

The costs of conflict can be so enormous that even some improvement must be worth having.[1]

THIS BOOK IS ABOUT CONFLICT and how to resolve it. Conflict comes in many guises and manifests itself in many different ways, but we all know what it means to lose our inner peace. Whatever our background, whatever our culture or age, we have this in common: we know what it means to be hurt by conflict. Sometimes we have lost and lost badly; sometimes we have won and won triumphantly; but most times—win or lose—we have hurt and been hurt. Conflict and suffering are inseparable partners.

My prime purpose in putting this book together is to provide a clearer understanding of the processes of conflict, reconciliation and peacemaking in order that you may reduce the level of hurt as a result of the growing conflicts of our world. Industrial manager, educationalist, church leader, social worker, parent or single—whatever your context, conflict is part of your world. This book is for all of us.

Peacing Together is a practical book. I have attempted to bring together such wisdom and experience as I have gained in the course of my activities as a problem-solver, counsellor and mediator; and to be honest, I must also add my experiences as a conflict-maker—planned and unplanned! In

9

reading *Peacing Together* you will discover techniques for handling conflict, reconciliation and peacemaking and at the end will be better equipped to handle conflict—your own and that of others—and to bring and know peace. But one book is not enough to make a lot of difference to the rising tide of conflict. What this world needs is men and women who are prepared to live as peace-bringers. Only by actively 'peacing together' can we make a real difference to the level of peace in our communities. The difference, though small today, can make all the difference in the world tomorrow.

'Peacing'?

I had some difficulty in arriving at the title *Peacing Together*. The English language is rich in words relating to conflict— we have words such as 'fight' and 'fighting', 'war' and 'warring', 'conflict' and 'conflicting', 'battle' and 'battling' and so on—all nouns with their accompanying verbs. But we have no verb in English to correspond to the noun 'peace'. For us, peace is a state, not an act. We don't 'do peace'. But this book is about doing peace. It is a guide to action for peacemakers, and I could find no word that satisfactorily captured the concept, so I have taken the liberty of creating a new one—*peacing*.

Peacing is a high-risk business. The forces that seek to divide, as we shall see, must not be underestimated. The lone peacemaker is too vulnerable, too exposed and under too much pressure to survive long in the midst of damaging interpersonal conflicts. Peacing is, then, a team game, to be done with the support of others. So *Peacing Together* will encourage you to revise your ideas about conflict and reconciliation and to work with others in new ways to bring a greater degree of stability and peace to the lives and organisations of those around.

Conflict

Conflict is an emotive subject. Passions are aroused; anger and fear cloud our thinking; ill-considered words and actions result in regret, remorse and guilt, and trap us into a state of helpless subjectivity. It is because we tend to lose our objectivity in conflict that I have attempted to approach the subject in a logical and dispassionate way. Although conflict is an experience common to us all, and some people even enjoy it, few people today clearly understand the origin, nature and—more importantly—the process by which conflict can be increased or decreased. *Peacing Together*, therefore, will help you come to grips with this universal, yet misunderstood phenomenon we call 'conflict'. We shall also examine our personal approaches to conflict. What do we do when faced with a conflict? What should we do?

As we shall see, there is a number of ways to respond to conflicts; not all result in peace, and even some peaceful outcomes are not necessarily desirable. Peace falls on the battlefield after the last resistance has been overcome. Peace descends on the family after the divorce papers are finalised. Peace rests on the empty factory after the confrontation of management and union has bankrupt the business. These forms of peace are common in our society, but they do not represent the peace that comes from reconciliation, which only comes about when we approach a conflict in a very special way.

Reconciliation

Reconciliation has to do with the restoration of unity and harmony, not simply the cessation of hostilities. Put so simply, the difference is obvious; but what actions have to be taken to ensure that the difference becomes a more common outcome of our peacemaking efforts? With this question in mind I have set out guidelines for reconciliation based on some age-old, yet too often neglected, principles and practices. The guidelines suggest how reconciliation can become more the norm in any divided community— church, family, business or society.

But a word of caution is needed here. No change in relationships can take place without effort. Effort requires energy, and energy is expensive—it uses up resources. To transform a conflict into peace requires effort—so who supplies the effort? Who provides the energy, and who pays the price of the peace? I believe one reason why conflict is on the increase in our communities is that fewer and fewer people are prepared to pay the cost of reconciliation. Therefore, for those engaged in recreating harmony, it is important to recognise that there is a cost, and that we are required to pay some of that cost from our own resources. In the final chapters of *Peacing Together* I will deal with the issue of how to keep our own peace while working as a peacemaker for others.

The periods of our life when we are free of conflict are increasingly rare. More and more we seem to be faced with parties in conflict—departments in our organisations, children in our families, groups in our churches and factions in our communities. If we are to avoid tearing ourselves and our society apart, we need to do more than simply try to hold things together and patch over the threadbare fabric of our strained relationships. We need to become skilled, active peacemakers.

Peacemaking

Reconciliation and peace are not the normal consequences of conflict; in reality, the natural outcome of conflict is more conflict! *Peacing Together* provides ways to recognise conflicts earlier and suggests strategies and tactics to prevent destructive escalation. Sadly, not all our efforts at reconciliation will be successful. Some parties will be set on a course of self- and mutual destruction and will not be able or willing to change. Jesus Christ, the great reconciler, was unable to bring peace to the city of Jerusalem despite his many attempts. We shall look at some of the reasons for the breakdown of the peacemaking process later.

One of the best-known comments on peacemaking comes from the famous prayer of St Francis of Assisi:

Lord, make me an instrument of thy peace;
Where there is hatred, may I bring love;
Where there is injury, may I bring pardon;
Where there is discord, may I bring union;
Where there is error, may I bring truth;
Where there is doubt, may I bring faith;

Where there is despair, may I bring hope;
Where there is darkness, may I bring light;
Where there is sadness, may I bring joy.

Oh Master, make me not so much to be consoled as to console;
Not so much to be loved as to love;
Not so much to be understood as to understand;
For it is in giving that one receives;
It is in self-forgetfulness that one finds;
It is in pardoning that one is pardoned;
It is in dying that one finds eternal life.[2]

Yet despite the undoubted importance of the role of mediators in society, it is obvious that there are dangers to those who seek to bring peace: 'Blessed are you when people insult you, persecute you and falsely say all kinds of evil against you.'[3] No, peacemakers are not always loved or valued. This is one of the costs of peacemaking, and the price is high—too high to be paid alone. As we have already noted, peacemakers need support: a network of friends, colleagues and partners in peace who will provide the care, maintenance, and energy renewal needed by those who would stand in the front line of the battle to bring about reconciliation.

Have you a small, close group that you can count on for support when the conflict gets rough? In my book *Seconds Away!* I devoted a chapter to this need for us all to have a small, intimate group of people whose personal support we rate as being of high value to us, and who in turn regard our support as of high value to them.[4] One of the priorities for the would-be peacemaker is to create this sort of support. Who would constitute such a group for you? Two or three people would be sufficient. As you begin this book, you could benefit from having someone read it with you. Learning together helps objectivity and is more fun. The relationship would also be strengthened, and you could face the challenges of peacing together—together!

So let us now move on to consider what is happening in a world that talks peace but experiences only conflict.

CHAPTER ONE

THE WORLD OF CONFLICT

We see by the light of a thousand years
And the knowledge of millions of men;
The lessons they learned through blood and in tears
Are ours for the reading, and then
We sneer at their errors and follies and dreams,
Their frail idols of mind and of stone
And call ourselves wiser, forgetting, it seems,
That the future may laugh at our own.[1]

LASTING PEACE remains a persistent yet illusive dream. For any of us to hope to take successful action against the twentieth century's rising sea of troubles must seem foolishness indeed. Yet it is from this undeniable desire for peace that we can take courage. The ability to change our behaviour is part of our human condition, and we can take action born of that persistent dream of peace, despite the overwhelming growth of conflict in our world.

More than any other, this century seems to have been filled with treaties, truces and peace talks. Perhaps historians would tell us that we are no different: nations have always talked peace then gone on to war. It seems that mankind knows only two states — war and preparation for war. 'Peace in our time' has become a term of mockery and contempt. No significance will be placed on the next cease-fire announced in Lebanon. We have grown weary of the failure of peacemakers. The conflicts in Ireland are still very much with us; the Palestinian problem remains unsolved despite exhaustive efforts by many parties.

Hostilities will not go away in our lifetime, yet our great expectations of world peace and harmony and unity will not go away either. This gulf between reality and our dreams mocks us as we see so many relationships torn apart by escalating conflict. And when, occasionally, peace is restored to some strife-torn land or city in our world, it is the forced peace of control and oppression. Fear keeps the parties from open confrontation, yet each continues to eye the other warily from prejudiced positions across barricades, and each sleeps uneasy in vulnerable beds. This is the age of peace when there is no peace.

How have we come to this state? What decisions, what policies, what actions have brought the human race to the point of self-destruction? And what of the future—must we continue to live in fear of our neighbour?

Back to the Beginning

If we are to deal with present-day conflict and equip ourselves for the seemingly inevitable conflicts of tomorrow, then we must understand that peacemaking requires a hard-nosed realism.

From the earliest recorded times man has sought to explain the overwhelming presence of conflict in the world. The mythology and lore of many cultures place the origins of conflict among the gods themselves, with the eternal struggles spilling over into the world and lives of mortals. The Judeo-Christian worldview is in some ways similar— there is a battle taking place between spiritual powers, and we are caught in a part of it. 'For our struggle is not against flesh and blood, but against the rulers, against the authorities, against the powers of this dark world and against the spiritual forces of evil in the heavenly realms.'[2] The prophet Isaiah, too—writing almost 3,000 years ago—described a rebellion in heaven, the results of which 'laid low the nations'.[3] Where this event stands in the history of the world is not clear, but the Bible does make clear the growing nature of the process of conflict in our world.

The Growth of Conflict

We can see a steady growth in conflict over the millennia in the writings of the Old and New Testaments. From the tranquillity of Eden's tree of life in Genesis, to the eternal peace of God's new city in Revelation, lies a path of ever-increasing conflict. It is important to see today's conflicts in the context of this historic and future pattern, so let us consider for a moment the picture that emerges when we look over the human track record.

INNER CONFLICT

Ancient literature and folklore from all around the world point to the destructive yet creative effects of conflict, whether between the primeval elements of earth, air, fire and water, or in the struggles between the deities and powers. Whatever the nature and form of the conflict, the storytellers of old were careful to emphasise the origins of conflict as being *within* the warring parties. The same is true for the human race; conflict has its roots within us. Consider for a moment the universally well-known story of our first parents, Adam and Eve.

In the garden of Eden, Eve was made aware of a choice, one which involved irreconcilable tensions—to believe what her God had said, or to yield to her own desires to be different. The conflict was not between her and the Tempter; rather, it was between what she was and what she might become. It was an inner conflict. Most conflict is 'inner conflict'. It causes more stress and more hurt than all the physical forms of conflict put together, and it affects us all. It is the battle that rages within us, and its roots are desire, selfishness and fear. Its weapons are psychological and spiritual, and we are the casualties: we lose peace; we lose confidence; we lose sleep; we lose health, and eventually—if the inner struggles are not checked—we may lose our sanity and our very life.

Inner conflict is the major source of mental, spiritual and physical sickness of our day. The links between the physical and the psycho-spiritual states of the individual are only now being rediscovered by Western medicine, but such links have long been recognised in the East.

> ...in sickness be not negligent. Pray unto God, for he can heal.... And also give a place to the physician. And let him not be far from you, for there is indeed need of him, for there is a time when success is in his power.

So counselled Jeshua Ben-Sir in the second century BC.[4] The formula has not changed. To be whole, to be healed, to be at peace—we need the touch and word of forgiveness. (Graham Greene's novel *The End of the Affair*, for one example, illustrates the powers of touch to heal both physically and spiritually.) As we come to know forgiveness and emotional healing, so we can also be healed in our bodies. While the world concentrates on the outward manifestations of conflict, it remains to those of faith to bring peace to the ravaged battlefields of the heart by proclaiming the power of forgiveness to bring peace. We will look later at this inner conflict to rediscover the paths and processes of reconciliation.

INTERPERSONAL CONFLICT

The silent and secret wars of the inner being will, if left to rage unchecked, break out into overt aggression towards others. In the earliest scriptures, the effects of Cain's disappointment and anger burst forth in violence against himself and his brother. In ancient Greek legend, too, is recorded the mythological struggle between Zeus, later the father of the gods, and Saturn, one of the great elder gods. Man against man, man against giant, man against his god —ancient writings are full of such accounts. The stage is set, the example is given, and succeeding generations give continuing testimony to man's inhumanity to man.

Figures for offences against the person are rising steadily in most Western societies, and many inner cities have large 'no-go' areas after dark. But the threat is not to the individual alone. History is full of examples of the fate of societies which lost their sense of value of the individual; Roman, Aztec, Mayan and many others crumbled as human life became expendable in sacrifices, games and entertainment. Nearer to the present day, the Third Reich, Stalinist Russia, Biafra, China of the Red Guards and dictatorships of all politics and colours have continued to use violence as a tool of the state.

In their challenging book *Whatever Happened to the Human Race?*, Francis Schaeffer and Everett Koop set out the catalogue of conflict and violence which not only pervade our nations, but are condoned and supported by them. People say, 'My rights are not your rights, but I am stronger, so you must lose.' 'I am a woman, you are only an unborn child.' 'I am a man, you are only a geriatric burden on the family.' 'I am whole, you are deformed, disabled, different.' On every hand people define their rights and then proceed to impose them on others. The dedication of this thought-provoking book is 'To those who were robbed of life, the unborn, the weak, the sick, the old, during the dark ages of madness, selfishness, lust and greed for which the last decades of the twentieth century are remembered.'[5] Published in 1980, the text is a largely unheeded warning to Western society, which now has the shame of the tragic statistic that the most dangerous place to be in the United States is a mother's womb! In the United Kingdom, social services are stretched beyond their limits; prisons are overcrowded by a factor of more than 200 per cent; child abuse and attacks on the elderly, sick and defenceless increase. In just over a generation, crimes of violence have increased by 300 per cent. Clearly the level of violence cannot continue to rise and our nations remain intact. But what can be done? In particular what can be done by today's church? The reports of the Archbishop of Canterbury's Commission on Urban Priority Areas (later also on rural areas) make gloomy reading; nevertheless they represent attempts to face up to the growing problem of the increasing frailty of civil order and its accompanying interpersonal violence.[6] And subsequently the Church Urban Fund, launched in spring 1988, has promoted action and raised society's consciousness generally.

FAMILY CONFLICT

The next level of conflict reveals itself as the one-to-one aggression characterised by the violence of Cain and Zeus which has grown to embrace the enlarged family or clan. With Abraham and Lot—uncle and nephew—the issue is one of resources. As members of one family they get along fine, but they are competitors in the same business: both need the water, and both need the grazing. Yes, members of one family should stick together; they should all be friends. But often, the house is not big enough for all of them; someone has to go, or ambitions have to be modified. The potentially destructive conflict in this Genesis story is avoided by each going his own way.[7] (Avoidance may bring peace, but it does not bring reconciliation.)

Similarly, in Shakespeare's *King Lear*, the same kind of family conflict arises as Cordelia, the king's youngest daughter, refuses to flatter her father as her elder sisters have done. In the end, as the conflict escalates, the whole family is destroyed by Lear's insatiable desire for flattery.

Living in close proximity to others requires us to be sensitive to the needs of those around, to be less willing to stand up for our rights in the face of pressure on our boundaries. Yet there is a limit to this sensitivity. There is a limit to the space we can give others before the pressures on our own family become unbearable. Economic pressures come with unemployment, debts, repossessions, evictions, inadequate diets and insufficient heat; all these bring our families into conflict. Social pressure from poor housing standards, breakdown in the law and order in our communities, increasing isolation for many groups, including the disabled, the elderly and the ethnic minority —these, too, are sources of conflict for our families. Sensitivity to others' needs helps, but it is not enough, for the conflict that arises from the failure of expectations, the loss of self-esteem, and the social stigmas which accompany poverty and deprivation will not be removed by sensitivity; social action is needed on an enormous scale.

The statistics speak for themselves. Divorce, single-parent families, teenage suicide, drug abuse and alcoholism all point to families in torment, while between families, tolerance and neighbourliness decline. 'One of the problems is that . . . families who are internally disorganised and chaotic . . . create chaotic social conditions which in turn further disturb individuals and their families.' So states the Family Welfare Association in its submission to the *Faith in the City* report.[8] A spiral of conflict which cannot be broken by individual social responses alone has been established in the modern family.

A Spiral of Conflict

—*Threat* to the individuals within the family from destructive social forces leads to

—*Pressure:* the stress that comes from fear and uncertainty and causes the individual to seek to destroy the sources of threat, so

—*Conflict* develops: husband against wife, father against son, children against parents. The fabric of the family degenerates, and

—*Disorganisation* ensues as communication breaks down and relationships deteriorate. Eventually the family unit fails and

—*Disintegration* results, socially, spiritually and physically; children are taken into care, homeless, bewildered and

angry. This anger affects those around and results in
— *Escalation* of the problem—those who are hurt begin to hurt
others and become part of the ever-increasing barrage of
destructive forces.

Let me illustrate this spiral from a case among many in
my counselling work. Mike was in care in a children's
home. He was intelligent, articulate and good at sport but,
at fourteen, was in regular trouble with the police and other
authorities. His father was in prison for robbery with
violence; his mother, unable to cope with the children on
her own, had put the three eldest into care five years earlier.
Mike had been the product of a threatened, pressurised,
disintegrated family. Now at fourteen the process was
escalating. He had been expelled from school and was
creating such chaos in the home that he was threatening
the fragile stability of the other children. He could not be
trusted to take part peaceably in any social activity.

Mike was and still is and always will be a product of this
circle of conflict. There are more and more Mikes being
created every day. A spiritual initiative is needed. How
many families do you know who are in the grip of conflict?
The statistics of the family in Britain in 1988 are quite
frightening—one marriage in three ends in divorce,
according to the 1984 Office of Population Censuses and
Surveys. What initiatives can we take? The family is God's
institution; the church is his instrument of healing. Where
then are the processes of reconciliation? Where have all the
peacemakers gone? Probably to church, but it is in the
high-rise flats, in the streets, in the houses that the peace is
needed.

INTERGROUP CONFLICT

Conflict between groups is nothing new. Greek legend
recalls the hideous battles between the Titans and the gods;
the scriptures describe the jealousy of those around him
aimed at Jacob the Patriarch; and British coastal towns in
the 1960s witnessed skirmishes and outright battles
between the Mods and the Rockers. On all sides people
group together and declare their position, whether it is

union versus management, or black versus white, or opposing football supporters, or political activists, or terrorists, or freedom fighters—each declares the right, and each declares the others to be wrong.

Within the church it is liberal versus fundamentalist, charismatic versus traditionalist. Wherever you can define a group, you can also define a boundary, and where there are boundaries there is the potential for conflict. For groups do not only bring people together, they also divide. Today's proliferation of 'freedom fighters', so called, is one indication of just how ready people are to engage in and encourage others to engage in conflict. The power of the group to bring out both the best and the worst in people is remarkable. (The 1988 street battles between soccer hooligans is just one evidence of a force at work in groups which seems to remove all sense of restraint, dignity and humanity.)

Developing team spirit may be viewed as a positive way of reducing the potential for conflict between individuals, but it is also one of the major factors contributing to violence on the intergroup level. By creating a team we develop loyalty, vision and identity—laudable in themselves, but they are exclusive. When set against other loyalties, other visions and other identities, they become sources of conflict and destruction. The church has been slow to understand the nature of teams and groups and is only in recent times rediscovering the meaning of team ministries and the dynamics that accompany them. But it is still a long way from coming to grips with the problems of intergroup conflict. This is one reason for the growing number of splits in churches and the proliferation of new sects and denominations.

Where are the intergroup conflicts in your life? Beyond a team lies the possibility of creating a community—the process of building bridges between groups within a society or organisation. We struggle with this because we have not yet learned to deal effectively with the inner and interpersonal levels of conflict.

CITIES IN CONFLICT

As early as 2000 BC, a pattern of inter-city warfare was established. Such conflict was to be a major feature of the world for many turbulent centuries: the Trojan wars, the Carthaginian wars, the struggles between the city states of Italy, and the battles between king and parliament in England all testify to an extended period of inter-societal violence. For 400 years the border towns of northern England and southern Scotland were in a state of continuous conflict. Today, such inter-city conflicts have been reduced mainly to sporting events and competition for investment, industry, tourism, etc. Yet the seeds of conflict remain, and the phenomenon of the city divided against itself is becoming more common again, whether that antagonism takes the form of sectarian divisions in Beirut and Belfast, or racial division in Liverpool and London, or the economic divisions of the pavement and slum-dwellers and the middle-class residents of Rio de Janeiro and Calcutta. It is clear that mankind's more recent history has been one of growing inequality—in lifestyles, income, housing, education, public services and the general level of public amenities. Increasing inequality must inevitably lead to the polarisation of peoples and cities. Such a polarisation cannot go on for long without civil disturbances on a wide scale. This is not a political statement: it is a sociological one. Society cannot deprive most of the people most of the time for ever; sooner or later it will have a revolution—be it in Brixton or Toxteth or Soweto.

Cities are central to the future of this world. In 1900 some 15 per cent of the world's population lived in cities; by 1950 this figure had risen to 30 per cent; and by the end of the century it will have reached an estimated 60 per cent—more than half the world's population living in environments which even now are breeding increased violence, stress and conflict.[9] We have little time left to find ways of reducing the personal and environmental forces which cause the escalation of conflict in our cities.

INTERNATIONAL CONFLICT

This text is not intended primarily to deal with conflict at macro levels; nevertheless, it is important to note the increase in potential for conflict at a world-destroying level, for the overall climate of hostility and mistrust influences the way we view conflict and its legitimacy. Fed on a diet of TV violence, bombarded with daily examples of verbal conflict between national political leaders and desensitised to the true hurt and cost of conflict, little wonder that we resort to violence first rather than last.

The period of relative 'peace' the world has experienced since 1945 is one of the longest since the Middle Ages. But the absence of *full-scale* international conflict is hardly a sign of true peace. The Pol Pot atrocities and the genocide of the Khmer Rouge more than surpassed the horrors of the Nazi holocaust and it is also true that each of the world powers has been engaged in 'limited conflicts' during the past ten years—the Gulf, the Falkland Islands and Afghanistan—while Central America, Africa, the Middle East, India and Indonesia have all been shaken by minor but nonetheless deadly discords. International spending on arms continues to rise; the race has now been taken beyond the confines of the earth into space itself. We have come a long way from Cain and Abel—or have we? Surely the sources of the conflict are still the same. Do we not still want to be different? Do we not still envy others? Are we not still willing to deceive and take from others what we desire—by force if necessary? Do we not still live in fear of our neighbour? Unfortunately the answer to all these questions is 'yes'. We may have come a long way, but the long path has been one of growing conflict. And for the future?

SPIRITUAL CONFLICT

One writer reminds his readers that the real conflict is not physical. Despite all that we see around us, despite all the focus on social confrontation—whatever the level—the real battle is a spiritual one. All conflict—from inner conflict to cosmic—is spiritual and will increase. Though this

18	I am divorced or separated.	5
19	People say I am a critical person.	2

Subtotal B _____

20 Score 1 point for *each* close friend or relative who has been divorced in the past two years.
21 Score 1 point for *each* endorsement on your driving licence.
22 Score 5 points if you or one of your immediate family has spent time in prison in the last five years.   5
23 Score 10 points if you or one of your immediate family has attempted to commit suicide in the past five years.   10

24 Do you find that people bring you their family problems?

Almost every day	5
Frequently	4
Sometimes	3
Rarely	2
Never	1

25 Would you describe your family as:

A problem family	5
Financially troubled	4
Unhealthy	3
Ordinary	2
Happy	1

Subtotal C _____

Mark the appropriate points for each 'Yes' answer:

26	Do you belong to any sports club?	1
27	Do you belong to any societies?	1
28	Have you ever been expelled/banned/fired from a club or organisation?	2
29	Do you play competitive sports?	1
30	Are you a union member or a member of any management organisation?	1
31	Are you a member of a political party?	1
32	Have you ever campaigned to change the law?	1
33	Have you ever drawn up a petition?	2
34	Have you ever signed a petition?	1
35	Have you had personal contact with a disadvantaged family this week?	1

INTERNATIONAL CONFLICT

This text is not intended primarily to deal with conflict at macro levels; nevertheless, it is important to note the increase in potential for conflict at a world-destroying level, for the overall climate of hostility and mistrust influences the way we view conflict and its legitimacy. Fed on a diet of TV violence, bombarded with daily examples of verbal conflict between national political leaders and desensitised to the true hurt and cost of conflict, little wonder that we resort to violence first rather than last.

The period of relative 'peace' the world has experienced since 1945 is one of the longest since the Middle Ages. But the absence of *full-scale* international conflict is hardly a sign of true peace. The Pol Pot atrocities and the genocide of the Khmer Rouge more than surpassed the horrors of the Nazi holocaust and it is also true that each of the world powers has been engaged in 'limited conflicts' during the past ten years—the Gulf, the Falkland Islands and Afghanistan—while Central America, Africa, the Middle East, India and Indonesia have all been shaken by minor but nonetheless deadly discords. International spending on arms continues to rise; the race has now been taken beyond the confines of the earth into space itself. We have come a long way from Cain and Abel—or have we? Surely the sources of the conflict are still the same. Do we not still want to be different? Do we not still envy others? Are we not still willing to deceive and take from others what we desire—by force if necessary? Do we not still live in fear of our neighbour? Unfortunately the answer to all these questions is 'yes'. We may have come a long way, but the long path has been one of growing conflict. And for the future?

SPIRITUAL CONFLICT

One writer reminds his readers that the real conflict is not physical. Despite all that we see around us, despite all the focus on social confrontation—whatever the level—the real battle is a spiritual one. All conflict—from inner conflict to cosmic—is spiritual and will increase. Though this world has seen a surfeit of struggles and is sick for peace, peace will not come until the Prince of Peace brings it with him.[10] But this does not mean that we despair or desist in our efforts to reduce the effects of the spiritual combat.

In Frank Peretti's novel *This Present Darkness*,[11] a small American town becomes the focus of an assault by the powers of spiritual darkness. Caught up by a desire for a kind of deep psychic and emotional perception, some of the characters have no idea at first that the net of evil is closing in to choke them to death. The power of evil is almost palpable in the novel, yet Peretti shows how the forces of light and goodness overcome and obliterate that evil through a few characters who dare resist it.

Peacemakers are the light of the world; they are that city of refuge that is set on a hill; they are the bearers of the peace of God. The world needs to see them, to hear them and to feel the power of the peacemakers: the children of God working with power for reconciliation in our generation.

Conflict Affects Us All

What then can we do? In later chapters of this book we shall consider the responses open to us all, but first we need a chart of the battle and a plan of the battlefield. We need a map that shows us where the major pressure points are in our own lives, as a result of the conflict around us. We will not be able to deal with conflict effectively in our own life or in the lives of others unless we are aware of the influences these conflicts have on us. Conflict is not simply out there but it is also in *our* world and in *our* hearts and minds.

'Man is born to trouble as surely as sparks fly upward.'[12] This was the comment of one early observer as he considered the effects of conflict on the life of one man. In the twentieth century we too are not immune to it. Conflict affects our attitudes, our health, our activities and our hopes. We must therefore ask ourselves some fundamental questions: How much conflict is in my own world? Is my private world disordered? Am I under pressure from surrounding and inner conflicts? If I am a victim of strife, then it is important for me to take steps to restore my own inner peace before I try to help others.

On the following pages you will find seventy statements and questions. Read through these and score yourself according to the answer that best suits your present situation. Explanations will follow when you have completed the checklist.

Conflict And You Checklist

Please respond to all questions and statements by circling the appropriate score.

			Score
1	I find myself feeling guilty:	All the time	5
		Frequently	4
		Occasionally	3
		Rarely	2
		Never	1
2	I experience frustration:	All the time	5
		Frequently	4
		Occasionally	3
		Rarely	2
		Never	1
3	I take sleeping tablets.		1
4	I suffer from high blood pressure.		1
5	I have difficulty in sleeping well.		1
6	Sometimes I cannot get my mind to switch off.		1
7	I have lost my temper more than once in the last week.		1
8	People would describe me as competitive.		1
9	I find it difficult to relax.		1
10	I am easily influenced by other people.		1
11	I am dissatisfied with my life at the moment.		1
12	I smoke.		1

Subtotal A _____

13	I have more enemies than close friends.	2
14	I have fallen out with a relative/friend/colleague/neighbour in the last month.	2
15	I have had a heated argument with someone in the last week.	2
16	I find some people really irritating.	2
17	I have been involved in violence since leaving school.	5

18	I am divorced or separated.		5
19	People say I am a critical person.		2

Subtotal B _____

20 Score 1 point for *each* close friend or relative who has been divorced in the past two years.

21 Score 1 point for *each* endorsement on your driving licence.

22 Score 5 points if you or one of your immediate family has spent time in prison in the last five years. 5

23 Score 10 points if you or one of your immediate family has attempted to commit suicide in the past five years. 10

24 Do you find that people bring you their family problems?

Almost every day	5
Frequently	4
Sometimes	3
Rarely	2
Never	1

25 Would you describe your family as:

A problem family	5
Financially troubled	4
Unhealthy	3
Ordinary	2
Happy	1

Subtotal C _____

Mark the appropriate points for each 'Yes' answer:

26	Do you belong to any sports club?	1
27	Do you belong to any societies?	1
28	Have you ever been expelled/banned/fired from a club or organisation?	2
29	Do you play competitive sports?	1
30	Are you a union member or a member of any management organisation?	1
31	Are you a member of a political party?	1
32	Have you ever campaigned to change the law?	1
33	Have you ever drawn up a petition?	2
34	Have you ever signed a petition?	1
35	Have you had personal contact with a disadvantaged family this week?	1

Your Experience of Conflict

INTERPRETATION OF RESULTS

Look first at your overall total and compare your score with the descriptions below:

5–35	Such a low score could indicate that you are somewhat disconnected from the real world. You may have real difficulty when you come to help others resolve conflict. Chapter Ten will help you.
36–70	Your world is fairly normal. You are acquainted with conflict, but it is not excessive. As you try to practice more peacemaking you will need to ensure that you maintain your own peace.
71–105	Some warning signals for you; the level of conflict in your life is high. You need to act to reduce it before you begin working with others.
Over 105	Your level of conflict is too high. At the moment you should concentrate on reducing it. Pay particular attention to this book as a means of tackling your own problems. Then, if you are successful, you can use your experience to help others.

If you scored over 10 in any one area, this is a sign that you need to concentrate on that particular area to keep your own peace; to guard against overexposure to conflict in this area and to work at keeping your own peace. Again, Chapter Ten will help you.

WHAT NEXT?

It seems certain that conflict will continue to increase. As you prepare to manage conflict better, it will be important for you to monitor the level of conflict you encounter daily. Remember, conflict hurts. How can you monitor conflict? One simple way is to keep a chart showing the times you have faced conflict and the times when you have been relaxed and at peace. The following chart is useful. Complete it for the last (or next) seven days—you'll be surprised! Conflict is stressful, and stress is one symptom of unresolved conflict.

	Sunday	Monday	Tuesday	Wednesday	Thursday	Friday	Saturday
High stress							
Medium stress							
Relaxed							
Peaceful							

Stress Levels

Think about the whole week. What do you recall—was it a stressful day or a relaxed day? Were there times of stress and peace? Draw a line which shows the pattern. Using this little chart you can monitor your time. Your aim should be to have more of your line below the mid-point and to keep it there as much as you can.

The big problem, as we shall see in Chapter Two, is that conflict usually gets out of hand.

Summary

In this chapter I have tried to show that conflict is endemic in our world. We all suffer from its effects, and we all contribute to its growth. Conflict will increase in our world. It may be that the threat of all-out nuclear war will retreat, but within our homes and communities we can expect to face more and more strife.

We will now look more closely at conflict, for if we are to deal with it, we need to understand it.

CHAPTER TWO

THE ESCALATION OF CONFLICT

Things fall apart; the centre cannot hold;
Mere anarchy is loosed upon the world,
The blood-dimmed tide is loosed, and everywhere
The ceremony of innocence is drowned;
The best lack all conviction, while the worst
Are full of passionate intensity.[1]

BILL WAS A CIVIL SERVANT, and Cynthia worked in the finance department of a large local company. They had no children, and their life seemed stable and fulfilling—until Paula arrived on the scene. Paula came on a transfer to Bill's department, and Bill offered her temporary accommodation until she found a place of her own. Bill's wife was delighted to have Paula staying. The young girl was a welcome addition to the household—at first.

I often had supper together with Bill and Cynthia, and soon Paula was a regular fourth member at the table. Then one evening as I was working outside, Bill came to the gate, and I stopped to chat. What began as the usual pleasantries about the weather and the vegetables soon turned into a serious disclosure. Bill was finding Paula's presence very disturbing. 'I can't get her out of my head,' he confessed. 'Do you think I'm in love with her, Dave?'

'Let's go for a walk' I suggested, and off we went down the summer lanes.

Bill was in great confusion. He felt torn apart by irreconcilable feelings for his wife and their guest. My first piece of advice was to see that Paula moved immediately. That way at least Bill would have some space without Paula in which to work through his feelings. Neither Cynthia nor Paula was aware of Bill's feelings—as far as he knew.

He took the advice, and Paula moved to her own flat within the month. But Bill's fascination continued to grow. Visits to Paula's 'to help her settle in' soon became noticed by Cynthia. A confrontation took place. Bill, still full of confusion, confessed to his feelings and committed himself to his marriage again—although at this time he had made no advances towards Paula. At one of our frequent suppers they talked about what had happened. On the surface it looked as though the relationship between Cynthia and Bill was settling down naturally, but Cynthia had plans. She felt very vulnerable with Paula still in daily working contact with Bill and was determined to remove the temptation from Bill's life completely. Her strategy was simple—make it so difficult for Paula that the girl would have to return home.

Cynthia then went to her own employers, her minister and her doctor. To each she told the same story of Bill's problem, but she described the effects on herself in very different ways and enlisted their help in writing to Bill's department head with their concerns. Cynthia also wrote to Bill's superiors.

The results were predictable—sad, but predictable. Paula was embarrassed and surprised by a relationship which did not exist in the way it was being described, but having been made aware of Bill's feelings by her boss, found in her own emotions an echo to his. Rather than be transferred again, she left and took another job locally. Her relationship with Bill grew, and so did Cynthia's anger and frustration.

Cynthia's next move was to inform the family, who came from all over the country to take sides in the struggle for the marriage. But the more others became involved, the less chance was there of bringing Bill and Cynthia together. After a prolonged, bitter and violent conflict that involved the families, the doctors, the employers and the church—Bill and Cynthia were divorced.

This story illustrates how conflicts tend to grow. As we noted in Chapter One, conflicts on the international level have been escalating over the centuries. The same growth is also evident in the conflicts we experience personally: suspicion leads to fear, fear to violence, violence to more violence. In marriages, in industry, in racial and religious intolerance—in cities, in neighbourhoods, in churches and families—the process is the same: conflict feeds on conflict. Even when we attempt to suppress it, either by force in the form of riot police, segregation or apartheid, or to conceal it behind a smiling mask, the conflict does not go away. It increases in intensity and will break out in more violent ways later, drawing in more and more people.

In this chapter I want to examine the process of conflict escalation. It is essential that the peacemaker be able to recognise the phase that any conflict between parties has reached, since how the conflict is defused will depend on the level of escalation. The time for the conference table is not 2 am with riot police on one side and terrorists on the other! If you arrived on the scene carrying a round table, you would probably be arrested for attempting to set up a barricade! Clearly there is a time when talking is not enough. Thus the peace-seeker needs to be realistic about the level and intensity of the conflict he is attempting to resolve.

We have seen how we all live in an environment of constant conflict, within and without. Fortunately people are able to contain most of these battles most of the time, and little damage is done, but when a conflict begins to grow, real problems arise. What causes conflict to increase? How can potentially dangerous situations be recognised early enough to prevent damaging confrontation and aggression? We shall look at these two questions now. (The processes of defusing conflict and restoring peace will be considered in later chapters.)

Three major phases are involved in the development of conflict:

—*Separation*, in which the parties emphasise the differences between themselves.
—*Divergence*, in which the parties strengthen their position and increasingly ignore any common ground or similarity

with 'the enemy'.

—*Destruction*, in which both parties close in and destroy each other.

The time taken to move from one phase to another may be a matter of minutes or may take a number of years. Let us look at each phase in more detail.

Phase One—Separation

DIFFERENCE

The fact that we are all unique gives us unlimited scope for focusing on the differences in all aspects of our lives. Physical differences alone—our height, our weight, our colour—give plenty of opportunity to distinguish ourselves from others. The colour of our skin does make a difference; prejudice, the ghettos, high unemployment and social deprivation are the experiences of many black people in the Western world, despite laws designed to prevent discrimination. Social differences are increasing, too. Accent, location, schooling, dress, interests, church—all serve as a means of differentiating between ourselves and others.

Spiritual and religious separation occurs as readily as the more outward manifestations of physical and social difference. Religious intolerance and persecution are quite common in Europe today, and not always is the minority on the receiving end. Often, in order to heighten their identity, minorities attempt to press their ways on to the majority. In some situations, immigrant religious groups practise their beliefs not only *in* but *on* the host culture in a way that would be impossible for Westerners living in countries from which these minority groups come.

But we need not cross religious heritage boundaries to find spiritual differentiation—Protestants and Catholics differ in Ireland, and in Scotland's cities most Catholic and Protestant children are still educated in separate schools. Meanwhile, in the Church of England and the Lutheran Church, the growing conflict over the ordination of women is distancing proponents and opponents. In the United States and the United Kingdom, ethnic churches are on the increase as Christians put distance between their own forms of worship and those of others of the same faith but of different culture or emphasis.

Neither is conflict limited to groups separated so obviously by their differences. We can be the same colour, culture and creed and still have scope for real conflict. We may have a different vision of the future. We may want to operate according to different principles. We may want to organise differently, to be hierarchical or egalitarian in our structures. We may want to pursue different priorities: defence before education, marketing before manufacturing, worship before evangelism, or physical needs before spiritual needs. In the end it all comes down to wanting to do things our own way, and so we distance ourselves. Whatever the focus of the difference, separation involves division, and in this first phase the emphasis is always on what we are (that they are not) and what they are (that we are not).

Let me illustrate phase one thinking from my own early experiences as a child in inner-city Glasgow. Whatever your own upbringing and origins, you will have experienced much the same. In the post-war years the sense of community was very strong in Britain's inner cities. In Glasgow the social architecture was built around the concept of the tenement and the 'close' (ie the inner stairs of the tenements that gave access to between eleven and twenty flats). The building's structure led to the development of close-knit community groups. By the time I was four years old, I already felt part of the eleven families from my close; knew by sight the hundred residents in our block. I also knew, although no one had taught me, which closes were 'good' and which were 'bad'. Areas and streets of the district were similarly labelled as being more or less 'desirable'. 'Those people in number 16 again. . .', 'Police in Victoria Road last night. . . .' Snatches of conversation and glimpses of knowing looks soon let any inquisitive child build up a picture of a world of differences: people who, somehow or other, were not quite like our family, closes and streets which were different from ours.

It was a fascinating world which had to be explored, had to be seen, had to be experienced! So the next day the information would be shared with the gang. 'Those people

in number 16 again...' and off we would all go down the
street to stand and gaze at number 16. We were always
disappointed! Number 16 was just like any other number,
the people coming and going had two of most things and
one of some—just like other folk. And the local youngsters,
who finally tired of our watching them, and who chased us
away, were just like us. On those nights we would go to
bed and think about the differences, reliving the watch on
number 16; and as sleep gently came, nightmarish horrors
would gaze out of the windows of that adult-condemned
residence—different.

School, when it came for me, was a great bridge-builder.
I actually got to sit beside a girl from number 16, and there
were boys and girls from Victoria Road. We all played and
learned together. Mothers would come and collect us at
four o'clock to escort us home. Wild with the energy and
enthusiasm of five-year-olds, we would rush out holding
the hands of our new-found friends, and mothers would
smile and nod and take us our separate ways as we shouted
our farewells to our new world as though it was a final
parting.

DISTANCE

The next day our mothers left us at the school gate with
'Now, remember what I told you.' What had we been told?
Well, it was about the folk from number 16 and how different they were. 'But Mum, they're not! And Mary's got a
puppy, and her big brother's in the army and has real
bullets and....' But it was no use. 'You must not play with
them, dear. Play with people from your own street.' So to
the difference was added distance. But you cannot keep
children apart for ever. The 'My mummy says I can't play
with you' is soon forgotten in the excitement of the playground, and for a while the power of the adult to differentiate and separate is broken, but only for a while. At four
o'clock segregation is reintroduced. Eventually, however,
the secret, sweet, clandestine relationship would be discovered.

DANGER

The secret note in the pencil case, the word from another mother in the close whose obnoxious sneak of a child reported everything—these were the informers, silent or aloud, who caused the next step in the escalation of the social war. Father would be informed. More reasonably, more gently—for he had fewer pressures on him—he would explain again the need for separation because they were different. But he had never played with them, had he? 'No, but what you don't understand is...' and there followed a long description of living conditions, values and something called a 'sanatorium' to which people from number 16 had to go, and I didn't want to go there did I? On further enquiry I discovered that the sanatorium was actually out in the country and sounded a very desirable place to be! Nevertheless, I had been introduced to the third part of the separation phase—fear. These people were dangerous, and I wasn't to play with them, use their combs (what self-respecting six-year-old would use a comb anyway!), wear their caps or visit their houses, closes or 'back greens' (as the squares of tarmac and cobbles behind the flats were called).

Little has changed in the forty years since my childhood. Parents of every generation encourage their children to be separate. But that is only the beginning of the damage, for in seeking to protect our children, we equip them to look for difference and danger in others. Thus we sow the seeds of division.

Within each phase, it is possible to identify a progression to the conflict. In the early stages of separation, the parties will be content to create distance. But eventually, if the conflict is allowed to develop, danger will be added to difference. Do not go near! Do not touch! Do not communiate! They are unclean, dirty—a threat to our very existence!

The realisation of danger represents a significant escalation, since in effect it puts the other party in quarantine. By such a step the parties effectively close off communication between themselves. They are now unable to hear or share a common ground or language. From now on feelings rather than fact will influence the course of the conflict. The step from seeing the opposition as *potentially* dangerous to seeing them as a threat is not a big one, but it is important. It is fear, then, which in part raises the level of conflict to the second phase.

Phase Two—Divergence

Although at the end of phase one the parties are clear in their own minds as to the identity and nature of the enemy, they are not yet ready to engage in all-out conflict. Phase two covers that period of preparation for confrontation in which the efforts of both parties are aimed at the strengthening of their positions. Although both sides may engage in talks or 'talks about talks', there is little or no intention of resolving the differences around the table. During this phase the prejudices of the separation phase will continue to deepen, and the distance between the parties will be further enlarged.

CREATING A UNITED FRONT

Conflict is hard on all parties. It is hurtful and costly in emotion and energy, so there must be a real commitment to the cause; the struggle must be worth it all. Thus, in this phase of conflict, parties are concerned to create unity within their number. Different tactics may be used, but the aim is the same—to heighten our belief in ourselves, our commitment to the rightness of our cause and the justice of our position. We are indeed right, and wisdom will die with us—but not during *this* conflict—because right and might are on our side!

As parties diverge, waverers are weeded out; those who talk of compromise or the consequences of failure are not worthy of our cause. Pressure to conform is high, and no questioning of the position, leadership or strategies is allowed. Outwardly and inwardly a united front is maintained as any reservations or misgivings are thrust aside. There is much evidence of this in the international and political worlds where government changes occur in rapid succession during preludes to war; the 'wets', who have no stomach for conflict, are eliminated or squeezed out.

MAINTAINING A GOOD IMAGE

A further concern is to ensure that others *see* the rightness of our position. Much talk takes place with third parties, observers, the press, friends and the world in general— anyone who will listen. They must know of the injustices we feel; they must understand the dangers of the enemy; they must be prepared for the action we will take. So we visit the United Nations and address the General Assembly; we visit our partners in Europe or the Warsaw Pact countries; we visit the so-called non-aligned nations and plead our cause. We may seek more than understanding— we may seek support for our position, for support is power (whether it is moral or military). We will talk to anyone— except the enemy. We will not have exchanges with them unless it is on our terms: a complete withdrawal, an unqualified apology or total capitulation. Why should we settle for anything else? Total victory is possible and is only a matter of time. Why consider compromise when we can win? I had learned these tactics long before I heard of the General Assembly of the United Nations or the Warsaw Pact.

As I matured through the classes at school, I became aware of an annual ritual of conflict. One Monday morning in our playground appeared a group of thirty large boys, large at least to us at eight years old; three years made a big physical and psychological difference. And these boys were obviously different: their uniforms were maroon and blue; ours were green and yellow. The playground was suddenly changed. Instead of running freely over our territory, we established no-go areas, where the intruders stood in defensive groups. They had come for the final term of their primary education from another school. A similar group would come each year and fuel this annual conflict. Uneasy suspicion would give way to sporadic outbreaks of fist fights, as our champions and bullies tested themselves against their champions and bullies. Our own differences would be forgotten, and our unity would grow. Plans would be made to settle scores, the last week of term would be one running battle in which many noses were bloodied on both sides.

PREPARATION AND POSITIONING

The preparations for that week were considerable. Timing, tactics and contingencies were all worked out. Without us knowing it, we were as boys being 'father of the man'. Our natural instincts prepared us for conflict in the playground in the same way as the generals of World War II, Korea, Vietnam, the Falklands prepared for their conflicts on a larger scale. At the international level, phase two ends when the parties position themselves for the first strike. Troops are moved up to the border; supply dumps are established; weaknesses in the enemy position are probed; the mode of attack is selected, and the time of D-day is set. At the interpersonal level we wait until we see the enemy in a vulnerable position, or we may attempt to provoke them into an ill-advised action, or we may decide that an early confrontation offers the best hope of success. Whatever the approach, we are now committed to actions designed to hurt and damage those who are against us.

Consider the following classic example of a fully developed phase two conflict. It was a sad situation. I was invited by a company's personnel director to visit a factory in the north-west of England. The problem as described to me was quite bizarre: of the seven members of the local management team, five had separated from their wives in the previous six months; two of these were suffering from nervous exhaustion, and two others were showing signs of alcohol problems.

It transpired that some years ago there had been a take-over of the local manufacturing site by a large international group. At the time of the 'merger', senior management on the site had been replaced by managers from the larger company. These men had held the local management together for several years. Then, three years before my involvement, a series of promotions had resulted in the formation of a new management team—some from head office and some old hands from the local site. The combination had been a disaster. Resentment was still high at the takeover. We/they thinking dominated, and now the conflict was running on full steam. Manager used every opportunity and every means to attack manager. Stories were spread; rumours and malicious gossip abounded. Factories might have walls, fences and gates, but these cannot contain interpersonal conflict. Suspicion began to develop at home, and the managers, under intense pressure at work, were unable to cope with the overspill of conflict into the family. For most of the managers the damage was already done before I arrived. Eventually all of them were removed, and a new team was introduced. Of the seven, I was able to help only two. The rest were unable to piece their marriages or careers together. Whether phase two conflict is crude or polite, it is very damaging.

Phase Three — Destruction

Phase three sees the parties locked in open conflict. A quick surprise attack may win a battle, but it rarely wins a war — the Falklands conflict, the Korean War and World War II all began with spectacular surprise assaults, but none of the initiators of these conflicts gained lasting benefit from being first to fire the shots. More often than not the first into the field have not thought through the strategic consequences of their actions and thus are not able to sustain their position in the face of a determined counter-offensive. But whatever the tactic, war has begun — though it may never be declared, as was the case in the Falklands conflict.

The longer the conflict continues, the more insensitive the parties become. Whereas they began with high moral words and principles, soon any action becomes justifiable. Conflict not only destroys people; it first destroys their values. Hence in World War II the British and their Allies for a long time condemned the indiscriminate bombing of civilian targets, but the bombing of Dresden as well as Coventry showed that eventually it takes more than moral values to inflict pain on the enemy. How long would the war with Japan have lasted, and how many more soldiers, sailors, and airmen's lives would have been lost had not the generals justified the civilian casualties of Hiroshima and Nagasaki as paying the price of peace? Eventually parties do use all the weapons at their disposal — gas, bacteriological, chemical and the other unspeakable horrors born of man's inner conflict. So, too, families and one-time friends tear their relationship and themselves apart in pursuit of victory.

In the final stages of conflict, the parties lose all their reference points: Christians act like demons; freedom fighters act like oppressors; and those who fight for peace learn only the skills of war. Mutual destruction is the end of all-out conflict. At the international level we live now with 'second strike capability'. Should *they* destroy *us*, from the ashes of our cities we will strike back to their destruction.

Whether between nations or within churches or families, phase three conflict is mutually destructive. It serves no good purpose. Even if it is seen as a way of resolving the continuing exchanges between two strong, opposing parties, phase three conflict cannot easily be contained. There is a saying in Swahili that when two elephants fight, the grass gets hurt. To engage in self destruction is evil, and it is worse to commit innocent parties to the same fate.

Think for a moment of your own conflicts. Look back to page 30 where you mapped out your own world of conflict. Are any of your conflict areas in the phases of divergence or destruction? What about your family, church and organisation? Are the conflicts out of control? The strife curve opposite illustrates the escalation process.

Summary

Left to themselves, parties in conflict tend to move up the strife curve, doing increasingly more damage to themselves and those around. This is particularly so when the parties are sure that they are right and that the issues at stake are important to them. Uncertainty reduces the tendency for escalation, while issues which are not important are regarded as not worth fighting over.

Before we go on to look at the origins of conflict, here is a short exercise on identifying the phases of conflict. Often the words used by the adversaries give clues as to which phase the conflict has reached. You might want to do this exercise with a family member or colleague who is also reading this book or as a discussion starter in a group.

The Strife Curve

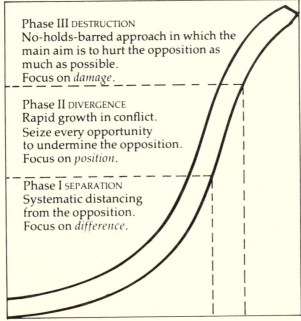

TIME

Below are twenty statements taken from typical conflicts. Each statement can be linked to one of the three phases: 1 separation, 2 divergence, 3 destruction. Read each statement and mark it 1, 2 or 3 according to the phase that it best fits. Of course the setting, tone of voice and accompanying non-verbal signals would influence your responses.

1, 2 or 3

1 'I don't care what it takes, I'll fix them!' _____
2 'We are all in this together.' _____
3 'What can you expect from people like that?' _____
4 'Just remember who you are speaking to.' _____
5 'Well, of course, she is from a single-parent family.' _____
6 'Be careful who you mix with.' _____
7 'You can count on my support.' _____
8 'We can win this one.' _____
9 'You asked for this!' _____
10 'I am not interested in what you think.' _____

11 'These deserve all they're going to get.' ___

12 'Give them enough rope and they'll hang
themselves.' ___

13 'They will do what I tell them.' ___

14 'I don't want you to be seen talking to them!' ___

15 'I'm not going to let her get away with that!' ___

16 'You can't trust a word he says.' ___

17 'I want nothing less than a full public apology.' ___

18 'It's them or us.' ___

19 'Aim! Fire!' ___

20 'Death or glory!' ___

CHAPTER THREE

THE ROOTS OF CONFLICT

What causes fights and quarrels among you?
Don't they come from your desires that battle within you?
You want something but don't get it.[1]

I T WAS MIDNIGHT. It was Africa. And it was hot. For a
week I had been investigating a conflict and had finally
found the roots of it. I had followed up a number of
leads in other countries and had uncovered bad
communication, inadequate management systems, cultural
differences, but all had proved dead ends. Although problems existed there, they were not bad enough to explain the
level of organisational conflict and stress. But here in the
noisy stillness which is the tropical night I sat opposite the
source.

The passionate intensity of his anger was quite tangible,
and wherever he had been in that organisation he had
carried it with him. He was a sower of division with a
pathological need to undermine authority. As we talked
the pieces began to fall into place — problems with previous
employers; conflicts in other locations; high dissatisfaction
among all his associates and further back to university,
school and home; evidence of deep-seated resentments
breaking out in acts of defiance and rebellion. The conflict
was not organisational, although the whole organisation
was suffering. The conflict was not interpersonal, although
many had become involved. Rather, the conflict was the

product of inner conflict. It wasn't a structural change that was needed in the company. It wasn't a change in the senior management that was required. Rather, an inner change was needed in the man who now faced me.

Walking Battlefields

It is said that it takes two to make a conflict, but as we are now beginning to see, that is not strictly true. One is sufficient. Each of us is potentially a walking battlefield of desires and counter desires. As we saw in Chapter One, the first recorded experience of conflict was as Eve struggled *with herself*. When we come to consider the processes for restoring peace, it is important to hold on to this fact that conflict comes from within us; it is not 'out there', it is 'in here'. If we focus only on the external manifestations of the conflict, rather than its internal origins, the results of our efforts to bring peace will be very limited indeed.

'You want something but don't get it,' warns St James as he considers the strife among the first-century Christians. This observation is crucial to our understanding of the roots of conflict. St James says it is our own desires that cause conflict; our aims and goals clash with the aims and goals of those around. I want what you will not or cannot let me have. This selfishness is at the root of all conflict.

There are two main elements to any conflict, namely the objective and the subjective. The objective element of the conflict consists of the facts of the situation — the fact that what you want is different from what I want. You want my position; I want a holiday in Greece and you want one in Finland. These objective elements can be stated, often measured — I am here, you are there. We can see the differences between us. But with these facts come the feelings — the anger, the resentment and the suspicion. It is these subjective elements which do the damage to our relationships, for even when the objective elements are resolved, the negative *feelings* often linger on as a potential source of future conflict. Thus if our own aims are the roots of our conflict, the emotions which follow as our aims are frustrated are the shoots which grow from the roots of selfishness.

Selfishness

This desire to have our own way at the expense of others is, quite simply, selfishness. In his *Lord of the Rings* trilogy,[2] J R R Tolkien masterfully creates an evil being whose one desire is to have power. The evil lord's strategy is to give ring gifts of great beauty and power which will eventually enslave the recipients. Throughout the saga the hero has to fight against the temptation to meet his own needs at the expense of others'. He triumphs in the end only because of his care for others' interests.

Tolkien's allegory captures much of today's real experience: our conflict has its roots in self-seeking, too. We too wish to impose our aims and beliefs on others. We too strive to advance our position and power without consideration for the needs of others.

But we cannot survive by mutual exploitation. We live in too small and fragile a world for us to ignore or steal from our neighbours. It was Jesus who summed up the commandment for harmonious living when he instructed his listeners to love God and their neighbours as much as they loved themselves.

We were not created for self—we were created for relationship. To enter into conflict with others puts us into a state which will damage us socially, spiritually, mentally and—if we stay in that environment long enough—physically too. Selfishness leads to fear—fear that our selfish acts will be exposed, fear that we might not 'win', or worse, fear that we might lose; fear that those around us will be more powerful in their selfishness and that they will do to us what we are trying to do to them!

Fear clouds our thinking, yet we continue to have moments of clarity in which our wrong attitudes and intentions cause us to know shame—shame at our self-seeking, shame at our greed. Guilt is almost sure to follow and to bring with it a sense of worthlessness, unworthiness and a loss of peace.

In such a condition we run the risk of becoming locked into a cycle of selfishness. In a vain attempt to rid ourselves of guilt we blame others for our discomfort. We reason this way: the reason we are feeling so bad is not that we are wrong in wanting things for ourselves. No, the reason is that other people are denying us access to those things which are right and proper for us to have! It is their fault that we feel so bad; it is their fault that the relationship has turned sour; they are the villains of our peace. Why don't they let us have what we want?

With the blame firmly fixed on the 'real' culprits, we can safely deny their right to be heard, to be valued or even to exist. They are wrong and should be punished. Since, of course, we are probably not in a position to punish them, then the best strategy is to avoid them—but then we will not know what they are up to! No doubt they will be scheming and planning against us. They are to be feared, and before we know it we are off on another trip of fear, shame, guilt, blame, denial and avoidance.

Frequent excursions of this nature will affect our sanity and our health. We need a way out of the vicious cycle of selfishness which lies at the root of all conflict.

The Cycle of Selfishness

The psychological 'fall-out' from the cycle of selfishness—like radiation—has long-term effects. Six of these negative side-effects are worth noting since the peace-seeker may have to give, or obtain, assistance in dealing with these persistent problems in the course of reconciliation. Even after the relationship has been restored, ongoing help may be reqaired to deal with the residual effects. The presence of these side-effects may also be the first signal that something is still not right in a relationship. Since *Peacing Together* is not a general counselling textbook, it is not possible to deal with these six problems in any depth. I will, however, refer to other material which might help you.

ANXIETY AND PHOBIAS

Conflict which results in an individual being locked into the cycle of selfishness may produce such an excessive fear of the other party that even the sight of him or the mention of his name triggers phobic reactions: sweat, anger, panic. In extreme cases the sufferer may go to great lengths to avoid any form of contact with the other party. Before any reconciliation is possible, the peacemaker has to help the person deal with that fear. Extreme reactions are not uncommon among people whose relationships and personalities are damaged, but in most conflicts, it is sufficient to remember that some fear is always present. The fear may be suppressed, denied or projected on to the other party, but it will nevertheless be experienced by both. With phase two and phase three conflict, a peacemaker is essential to help parties overcome their natural fear. As a relationship with and confidence in the peacemaker grow, the anxious parties will draw strength from the peacemaker and usually be able to overcome their feelings long enough for a meeting to take place. Face to face, but still feeling the protection afforded by the peacemaker, they can see irrational anxiety for what it is—a product of fear borne in the mind rather than based on any substance.

All parties should deal with anxieties and fears throughout the process of reconciliation. Failure to recognise and bring out anxieties will endanger reconciliation, which requires parties to take risks. In turn, anxiety makes risk-taking difficult, if not impossible.[3]

LOSS OF SELF-ESTEEM

Self-depreciation leads to feelings of inadequacy, inferiority and insecurity. When someone feels a deep sense of shame as a result, he tries to suppress the feelings. But driving them underground, as it were, usually results in a strengthening of the roots of conflict. The accompanying sense of worthlessness will prevent the parties from being brought together on an equal basis.

In the universally-known story of the prodigal son, the internal conflict of the younger son and the interpersonal conflict of the two brothers results in severe personal loss for the prodigal. Having wasted all his assets and been reduced to a down-and-out, he faces up to his situation. His shame leads to a lowering of his self-image. 'I am no longer worthy to be called your son,' he rehearses.[4] So he cannot go back as a son, but he still has some worth; he can work as a servant, if his father will have him. Had his self-esteem fallen until he felt he had no value at all, it is unlikely he would have set off for home. Reconciliation is very difficult when one party's shame is such that he experiences an absolute sense of worthlessness.

No matter how badly someone has behaved, he still has an infinite contribution to make to the future relationship. Without a contribution, nothing can be gained by reconciliation. A further problem arises when it comes to paying the cost of reconciliation, as we shall see in Chapter Nine. Someone who has a low view of self feels that he has nothing to pay—or more likely ends up trying to over-compensate, attempting to pay the cost for both.[5] But the cost of reconciliation must be *shared*.

DEPRESSION

This problem has many roots, only one of which is the guilt that comes from conflict. If the depression is linked with the particular event or attitude, the person 'feels bad' about himself. Someone suffering from this side-effect will be unable to take any initiative towards reconciliation for fear of rejection or failure.

Guilt has had a bad press in recent years. Many sociologists and psychologists have attacked Christianity as being the culprit in creating untold mental suffering born of unrelieved guilt. Certainly guilt can be destructive; yet it can also be the stimulus that leads to regret, repentance and reconciliation. Without a sense of guilt, there is no sense of wrong; without a sense of wrong, there is only the inflexibility that comes from being right. Guilt can provoke us to action, but it can also eat away at our confidence. Its relentless accusations can bring a deep sense of inadequacy and accompanying depression. Since we are unable to respond to the prompting of our guilt, our impotence fuels our guilt and increases our sense of helplessness. We are led relentlessly into despair, or we blame someone else.[6]

PERSECUTION COMPLEX

A person who frequently transfers the blame for this conflict to other people may in turn develop a feeling that he is being wrongly blamed. Even when no blame is actually expressed, the person may imagine plots and plans laid against him by others.

Recently I dealt with the case of a minister who had suffered a major heart attack and had subsequently undergone bypass surgery. He had been highly committed to his ministry, so much so that the church elders had become increasingly concerned for his health over the two years before his heart attack. However, their advice and counsel to slow down, accept more help and delegate more tasks had been rejected. Worse, the minister had accused the eldership of trying to undermine his authority. Faced with this, the eldership backed off and sought to support the minister more discreetly.

After the operation, with his activities severely (and perhaps permanently) curtailed, the minister was blaming the church and its leadership for his condition. Every move made by the church to try to support the minister was interpreted by him as a none-too-subtle attempt to undermine and 'get rid of him'. His doctor warned him that his recriminations were retarding his recovery, but he only rejected the doctor as part of the 'plot'. The patient redoubled his efforts to regain full health and began taking exhausting exercise to become fit again and take over his responsibilities once more.

Within six months he was back in hospital, in intensive care. The shock of this second crisis caused him to rethink. But, unable to see that the conflict was within himself, he was unable to change his behaviour or attitudes and did not survive. The peacemaker may have considerable difficulty with someone suffering from this form of paranoia since a peacemaker may be seen as part of the 'plot' to attack the sufferer.[7]

LOSS OF SENSE OF REALITY

Continual denial of a problem can lead to self-deceit and a refusal or inability to see things as they really are. The alcoholic is often the last to admit the problem. Committed to a course of action, the denier cannot admit failure and so attempts to filter out any information that might suggest that there is something wrong. (A major problem for Christian families and organisations, and others founded on a strong set of common beliefs, is that conflict strikes at the very heart of their concept of unity.)

A common response to the conflict is therefore to deny its existence: 'We are not divided! We are one!' Unable to admit their differences, they are unable to deal with them. The classic denial song 'Three Wheels on My Wagon' pictures wonderfully the capacity of some people to deny their problem. The wagon driver, pursued by Red Indians, keeps his spirits up in spite of losing a wheel in each verse of the song. The never-say-die pioneer is always capable of denying the realities of his conflict, and when everything is in flames around him, he's still singing cheerfully! Denial leads to the blissful sinking-ship syndrome. We may be going down, but we are sinking on an even keel!

The Babylonian Empire of King Belshazzar fell to the Medes and Persians because the Babylonian king refused to recognise the threat of the enemy armies surrounding his capital. Belshazzar feasted with his lords as the Medes tunnelled under the walls of the city.[8]

Denying a conflict's existence does not cause it to go away; forced underground, it will eat away at our foundations. The house—even a religious house—divided against itself will fall no matter how loudly it protests its unity. Thus reconciliation cannot be brought to people who do not see the need for it.[9]

WITHDRAWAL AND BURNOUT

Those whose main response to their hurt is to attempt to avoid its source may withdraw. Such people attempt to evade social contact and seek for security in seclusion. Clearly, withdrawal will create a barrier to reconciliation, since any attempt to bring the parties together will threaten the avoider's strategy. There is a phenomenon which increasingly affects those in conflict. 'Burnout' was first noticed in the helping professions—nurses, social workers, police and firemen—workers whose business brought them into close contact with other people's hurts and conflicts. The nurse who gives all her energies to the baby in intensive care only to see it slip irrevocably beyond the help of human technology and dedication; the policemen and the firemen who struggle for hours to free a smashed and trapped driver from a motorway pile-up only to pull a corpse from the wreck; the missionary who 'sacrifices' family, career and health only to experience complete failure (by human standards) in her mission, or to see her life's work go up in the smoke of persecution or rebellion—these are the casualties of other people's conflicts. Their sickness is now known as 'burnout'; the symptoms and behaviour are those of avoidance and withdrawal. Unable to cope with the personal consequences of other people's hurt, they suffer emotional and spiritual exhaustion, close in on themselves and attempt to withdraw from the hurting world. It is unwise to attempt reconciliation with people suffering from withdrawal until they have come to terms with their own hurts.[10]

The effects of prolonged, untreated conflict seem to be universal. Whatever the culture, whatever the age, the offshoots of the inner struggles are damaging. Most people

carry the scars from the battlefield of self. Not infrequently
we meet someone who would gladly resolve the conflict,
but the other party will not co-operate. In such circumstances the peacemaker's strategy, as when faced with any
of the offshoots, should be to help that person come to
terms with the reality, however painful, of his situation.

The following diagram illustrates the roots and offshoots
of the conflict. Its long-term effects on us can be quite
frightening.

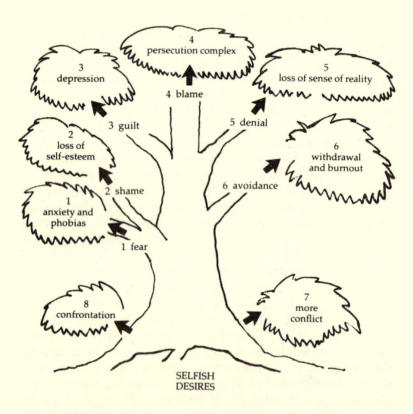

The Roots, Shoots and Offshoots of Conflict

Let us now return to the sources of conflict. These may be understood better with the help of symbolism.

Symbols, Myths and Concepts: Ways of Understanding Inner Conflict

Universal acceptance of the reality of the inner conflict has been reflected over the ages in the symbols and myths used to capture the experiences of the human condition. In the Far East, the yin-yang symbol encapsulates the sense of light and dark, good and evil, male and female in all things.

Yin-yang

In this symbol we see the eternal struggle between the good and evil—the light that shines in darkness and the darkness that is not able to overcome it.[11] By this philosophy, no person is wholly good or wholly evil; good and evil are present in all of us. This is a helpful way to understand the roots of conflict, for it helps us retain our humility, our sense of perspective on our own faults and failings. By this concept we have the 'two' needed to make the conflict within us. By this philosophy, true enlightenment and peace come through acceptance of the two forces within. This idea has been translated into modern myth in the *Star Wars* film series, where the dark side of the Force is set against all that is good and worthy, but the real struggle takes place within the hero.

DUALITY

If the Greeks had a name for it, they also had a god for it. Particularly fond of biological engineering, the Greek mind created a staggering array of crossbreeds—men, gods, animals, fish, birds—you name it, they combined it! To help illustrate the continuing acceptance of the good/evil duality in man, we only need to consider two of the Greeks' progeny—the centaur and the minotaur.

The centaur—half man, half horse—represented for the Greeks the positive combination of man and beast. The rational man dominated the power of the beast and kept the forces of the beast under control. The light and dark of the yin-yang have been replaced by man and beast, but the idea of fusion is retained.

In *the minotaur*, the fusion was more sinister. Here the beast dominated the man. The combination of the bull's head and the man's body produced a creature of evil and violence. The man is dominated by the lusts and appetites of the beast; the dark side of the force rules. Not OK!

In these two mythical creatures we find two ways to view and use the powers within us. When we allow conflict to escalate we are giving the beast its head; when we seek to create peace, we are attempting to bring the beast into submission.

PARADOX

The symbolism of the East and the fantasies of the Greeks may seem a long way removed from our present-day concepts and values, yet on closer examination we can find some parallels. At the centre of the Christian faith is the reality and symbol of the cross. As a reality it was an extraordinary contradiction; the Son of God dying the ugly death of a common thief. Symbolically, too, the paradox faces us. 'Unless an ear of wheat falls to the ground and dies, it remains only a single seed. But if it dies, it produces many seeds.[12] The Christian has to 'lose his life to find it'[13] and 'is crucified with Christ'.[14]

But even in the new life, tensions still exist. St Paul is still conscious that the good he wants to do he cannot do, and the evil he does not want to do he does![15] The symbolism changes, no longer black and white or man and beast, but now old man/new man[16] and flesh/spirit.[17] The paradox remains and will not be resolved in this life. We are all conscious of this inner division, and for some of us the division is multifaceted; we are aware not only of the black and white but the multitude of hues of grey that make up our being:

> Within my earthly temple there's a crowd.
> There's one of us that's humble, one that's proud,
> There's one that's broken-hearted for his sins,
> There's one that unrepentant sits and grins.
> There's one that loves his neighbour as himself
> And one that cares for nought but fame and pelf.
> From much corroding care I should be free
> If I could once determine which is me.[18]

Saint or Sinner?

What this means is that I need look no further than myself for the sources of conflict. Conflict is not something someone forces on me. Conflict is an outward manifestation of what I am inwardly: a self-centred, selfish being. And when I meet another just like myself, then 'like poles repel', as the science master taught us! In conflicts there are no 'innocent parties'; both are guilty of attempting to pursue their own goals at the expense of the other. Both are guilty of allowing the dark side, the beast, the sinner, the old man, the flesh — to dominate. Both are at fault. There are no saints in the conflict business! As we shall see later in this book, this is crucial to our understanding of the reconciliation process, though it is difficult to accept. We would rather be faultless and blameless, so we develop ways of dealing with our own beast. There are five common approaches to our beast.

1   To project my beast onto the other party. 'You're the one who's losing your temper!'
2   To transfer the blame for the lack of control of my beast onto others. 'It's your fault I'm losing my temper.'
3   To rationalise my beastly behaviour. 'Any reasonable person could be excused for losing his temper here!'

4   To suppress the beast, lock it away and banish it from my consciousness. 'Let's change the subject.'
5   Deny that I have any beast at all. 'I have *not* lost my temper!'

PROJECTION

'It's not my fault; it's theirs.' Basically we want to see others as the villains of the piece. Scott Peck describes this as 'scapegoating'. He explains that people using this mechanism 'feel themselves to be faultless, it is inevitable that when they are in conflict with the world they will invariably perceive the conflict as the world's fault. Since they must deny their own badness, they must perceive others as bad.'[19] But in conflict it is essential that both sides recognise their own part in the strife before peace is restored. As long as one or both parties continue to blame the other as the cause of the strife, little progress can be made.

TRANSFERENCE

Another method of dealing with the beast is to blame someone else for the way I am. 'Yes, it is true, I am being aggressive, but I'm this way because of how my parents treated me when I was a child. So if you will stand aside for a moment so I can throw another punch...!' By this argument the individual accepts his conflict; he comes to terms with the beast because it's not his; someone else gave it to him — in this case his parents. For many people it is acceptable to be violent *as long as it is someone else's fault.*

RATIONALISATION

This approach also seeks to make the conflict behaviour OK. The actions are justified. In the face of the enemy it is acceptable to fight back. 'Given my circumstances, deprivation, disadvantage and general exploitation by others, violence is all that is left. What else do you expect? *Everyone else does it!*' This is perhaps one of the most difficult attitudes to deal with, for it *is* true that conflict is the norm in our societies. It *is* true that everyone else does it. It *is* true that exploitation and the denial of rights abound in our society. But it is also true that to respond by conflict simply worsens the problem.

SUPPRESSION

The surges of anger and frustration that often accompany a hindrance to our goals are reminders that the beast is alive and well and resides within. For some, the arousal of the beast is more threatening to themselves than the prospect of outward conflict, and therefore they try to suppress their feelings and force them from their awareness. Out of touch with their own emotions and feelings, they are incapable of dealing with the subjective side of the conflict. 'It doesn't matter.' 'I don't care.' 'She can do what she likes.' These are the words of the person seeking vainly to push the beast into oblivion. They fail to recognise their own true nature and are therefore incapable of establishing and maintaining lasting, healthy relationships based on who they are and what they feel. Suppressors need to get back in touch with their emotions if they are to deal effectively with the conflict.

DENIAL

The fifth typical approach to the beast is to deny that conflict exists — either within us or in our relationship with others. The denier will reconstruct and reinterpret situations, will insist that he is OK, and that nothing is wrong — or at least nothing is wrong with him!

SURRENDER

There is, of course, an alternative to all these: we can actually lie back and enjoy the beast — let it take over. After all, the beast is powerful, and it tends to get us what we want! We have already seen in this chapter that for such people conflict has become a way of life.

Taming the Beast

Recognising the beast within is not enough; we need to deal with it. In the New Testament, Jesus is frequently confronted by the evil spirits of wretched, beast-torn people. Often his first step in dealing with the evil is to identify it: 'What is your name?' he demands of the madman from Gadara.[20] He then moves on to cast out that evil. Similarly, in Frank Peretti's novel *This Present Darkness*, the men and women and angelic warriors who confront the evil in their town do so first by addressing them by name.[21]

We are responsible for our behaviour, whether it comes from our lighter or darker sides. We can only deal with our beasts through self-discipline and self-control. Taming the beast within us is not easy. As Jesus teaches his disciples to pray, he includes a prayer for deliverance from evil.[22] It is important to remember that evil is not only 'out there' but that it is in me. Later Jesus promises to his disciples the 'other comforter', the Holy Spirit who will come to stand with his followers in every trial and evil—teaching them to order the beast through the self-control he gives.[23]

Summary

If all this is true, then we can come to a general agreement on the roots and shoots of conflict. We can make some general statements about the origin, course and effects of conflict. We can say for example that:

1 Conflict is endemic in our society.
2 Each person is in part the source of his or her own conflict.
3 We tend to blame others for the conflict we experience.
4 The inner conflict is here to stay.
5 The Holy Spirit helps us in times of conflict.

The fourth conclusion might seem a bit worrying, but at this point we are only seeking to understand the nature of the problem. From Chapter Five to Chapter Nine we will consider how we might reduce the conflict, both internally and externally. At this point, however, we must conclude that the natural outcome of conflict is not peace, but more conflict.

CHAPTER FOUR

THE APPROACHES TO
CONFLICT

To be, or not to be: that is the question:
Whether 'tis nobler in the mind to suffer
The slings and arrows of outrageous fortune,
Or to take arms against a sea of troubles,
And by opposing end them?[1]

W E SAT TOGETHER in the corner of the coffee lounge of a large central-London hotel. He was the head of an international relief organi- sation. I was a total stranger to him but had responded to his request for a consultation to discuss the problems in his organisation. At sixty he was under a lot of pressure: working in the Third World is never easy for Europeans; but added to the challenges of the work there was wide-scale unrest in the organisation itself. Junior staff were criticising the leadership; instructions and decisions were being undermined, and anarchy was beginning. Since relief organisations work with minimum administrative and management staff, often with communication stretched way beyond its limits, it is relatively easy for large parts of any international relief organisation to take advantage of their own autonomy. The director had tried everything he could think of: he had tried appeasing the malcontents; he had tried giving the younger managers more responsibility; he had compromised on some issues and had fought on others. He now felt the only thing to do was to resign. He could not continue to live with conflict on all sides. Certainly the strain showed in his face and his mannerisms.

After listening to his problems, I asked him only one question: 'Do you think your work with this organisation is finished?'

He looked at me almost in astonishment and said with great conviction, 'No. There is much more that I could do!'

So I replied, 'Then stay and do it, but let's work out exactly what has to be done, and let's set goals for the unfinished business.'

We talked late into the evening and identified five key objectives. 'Those will take you five years to accomplish,' I continued, 'but with clear goals you can now begin to manage the conflict within the organisation.'

Six years later he retired, all five goals having been achieved. There was still conflict within the organisation, but it was being managed effectively and the organisation had never been stronger, nor its future brighter. For this man, the response to the conflict was to clarify his goals and to act in accordance with his vision. In effect, he took on the slings and arrows of outrageous fortune.

Not every conflict can be dealt with in this way. Often the other parties in the conflict are more powerful than we are. At such times a different approach may be needed. Over the years we develop preferred approaches to conflict, generally based on what works for us. Our parents, our teachers, our brothers and sisters, our bosses, our spouses — all of these have contributed to the formation of our preferred responses. Another critical influence will be our personalities: whether we are outgoing, articulate and competitive or whether we are retiring, taciturn and self-contained. Thus each of us usually has one or two standard responses to conflict. On the following pages a questionnaire will help you to assess your conflict approaches.

Your Approaches to Conflict

Below are five sets of nine statements. Read each set in turn. After you have read the first set choose three statements which are *most* like you, your attitude or your behaviour when you are in conflict and mark them with a tick.

Then choose the three which are *least* like you in conflict and mark them with a cross. Move on to the next set and do the same until you have completed all five. You will find it helpful to think of one part of your life — for example work, or family or church — when choosing.

SET A

1 I am fairly relaxed about life; conflicts do not bother me.
2 I believe in avoiding conflict whenever I can.
3 I believe that right will triumph eventually.
4 I can usually see the rights and wrongs on both sides of an argument.
5 I believe in 'give and take'.
6 I prefer to negotiate to get the best deal possible for myself.
7 Conflict should be faced.
8 I am usually determined to achieve my own goals no matter what the opposition wishes.
9 All is fair in love and war.

SET B

1 I am prepared to put up with a lot of criticism and opposition.
2 Most conflicts solve themselves given time.
3 If I believe I am right, I usually try to hold my position.
4 I believe in always being true to myself and my values.
5 A halfway position is usually acceptable to me.
6 In conflict, one side has to win.
7 When things are wrong I say so.
8 I will always try to win in conflict situations.
9 Attack is the best method of defence.

SET C

1 I believe survival is more important than principle.
2 If I am provoked, I try to ignore it.
3 I have a lot of patience.
4 I work hard to create good solutions acceptable to both sides.
5 I believe both sides should be prepared to make sacrifices.
6 If I have a good case, I try to win in a conflict.
7 I will take on anyone I think is wrong.

8 I believe in the survival of the fittest.
9 Compromise never solves conflict.

SET D

1 I'll go along with most people and situations.
2 Most differences are not worth fighting over.
3 If I am attacked, I tend to keep a low profile.
4 I am prepared to pay a cost to resolve a conflict.
5 I am always prepared to compromise if it means peace.
6 In conflicts, I take the opportunity to win as much ground as possible.
7 I always put all my cards on the table.
8 Conflicts are like competitions: there is always a runner-up.
9 If I show weakness, people will take advantage of me.

SET E

1 Anything for a peaceful life.
2 I tend to avoid aggressive people.
3 No one can force me to do things against my will.
4 Both parties need to be willing for conflicts to be resolved.
5 A bad solution is better than no solution.
6 I give away as little as possible in negotiations.
7 Conflicts between people should be sorted out as soon as possible.
8 I do not expect to win every conflict.
9 In conflict, might is right.

Later in this chapter, page 79, I shall interpret your responses, but for the moment, score each set according to the code:

2 points for each tick
0 points for each cross
1 point for each statement left unmarked.

Now place your scores in the following table. Enter your score for statement 1, Set A at the top of the column headed 1. Continue across the top of the columns for statements 2 to 9 from Set A.

Do the same for sets B to E, putting your scores for statements 1 to 9 across the table in the appropriate column.

When you have entered all your scores, total your scores in each column and enter the total at the foot of each column. Your overall total should be 45 unless you have missed a tick or cross.

SET	STATEMENT NUMBER								
	1	2	3	4	5	6	7	8	9
A									
B									
C									
D									
E									
TOTAL									

Scores from the Approaches to Conflict Questionnaire

The Options Available

Taking up arms against a sea of troubles was one option that faced Shakespeare's Hamlet, the Prince of Denmark, when the opposition began. This option is of course open to us today. Increasing conflict and violence in our society will sooner or later directly affect us, our family, our organisation, our church. Even now, as your own analysis shows in Chapter One, page 30, conflict is a real feature of your life.

It may be possible for us to ignore, avoid, or collaborate with the opposition to evade outright conflict, but occasionally we have to take on our enemies in direct, face-to-face confrontation. We will have to oppose them as St Paul was forced to do at Antioch with St Peter in the first century AD.[2] Certainly at the inner and spiritual levels of conflict we are encouraged to 'resist the devil'[3] and to 'take our stand against the devil's schemes',[4] though there are also times when we should not attempt to fight but run.[5]

What ways are open to us when faced with a potential

conflict? There are basically nine approaches. Remember that conflict arises from a selfish clash of wills—I want one thing, someone else wants another thing. Conflict may be over how we spend our money, use our resources and facilities, or over who should do what, when, how and where. On a larger scale, the desire may focus on territory, power or resources as one nation desires what others believe should not be theirs. Conflict therefore arises when the ambitions and goals of one party clash with the ambitions and goals of another. Thus we have our first option. Faced with a potential or real conflict we can either stick to our own goals—and our guns—and be as resistant as possible, or we can give up our own ambitions in the face of the opposition and help others achieve what they want, ie be co-operative. These two possibilities stand at opposite ends of a continuum.

How we actually co-operate or resist is important in determining the course of the conflict. For example, we can quietly state our position, saying that it is not negotiable, or we can use threats: 'If any attempt is made to alter the way we work in this plant, I will call for an all-out stoppage.' Or we may go as far as a pre-emptive strike. The Israelis intend to keep the Middle East free of nuclear power stations that have a capacity to produce fissionable material, so when Syria began to build a reactor, Israel bombed it before the station was working. Thus in relation to our own goals we can be either passive or aggressive in our approach. Again, these options stand at opposite ends of a continuum.

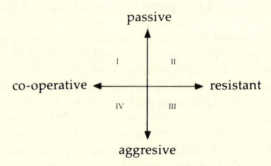

A Simple Conflict Approach Matrix

We can now illustrate the two lines together as axes to form a matrix showing four basic approaches:

These four approaches can be described as:

I The *collaborative* approach—characterised by passive co-operation.

II The *defensive* approach—characterised by passive resistance.

III The *offensive* approach—characterised by aggressive resistance.

IV The *confrontational* approach—characterised by aggressive co-operation.

We shall look at each in more detail before we extend the range of options.

THE COLLABORATIVE APPROACH

The passive co-operative approach to conflict is characterised by:

—Limited concern for goals by one party
—Strong concern for goals by other party
—A short-term focus
—An inequality of status and power.

Basically, collaboration requires one party to be prepared to yield ground. Collaboration is often the only route open when one party is significantly more powerful than the other. Collaboration is most commonly associated with the occupying forces in an overrun country, or when one person feels inadequate to pursue his own interests in the face of opposition.

Collaboration is usually a short-term strategy, for two parties cannot live together in peace for long when one is being denied the opportunity to work towards his goals. Nor can collaboration work for long when *both* parties suppress or suspend the pursuit of their own goals. This is clearly illustrated from coalition-type governments or joint ventures. The agreement is basically unstable and relies too heavily on constraint to be of lasting value. We agree to 'go along with them for as long as it suits us'. But without a unity of purpose, the relationship will be short-lived, for it favours one side rather than the other. Collaboration does not solve conflict; it suppresses it, for a time.

The alliance between the Liberal and Social Democratic Parties in the UK in the run up to the 1987 general election was a classic example of the collaborative approach. Both parties had to lay aside differences in order to appear a united alternative to the two major parties in Britain. Once the collaboration was seen to have failed, co-operation broke down and the two leaders pushed hard for their own goals—resulting in a breakdown in their relationship. Collaboration is the strategy of the short term, witness the short-lived coalition governments in Italy and Israel.

The strengths and weaknesses of the collaborative approach are set out below.

THE COLLABORATIVE APPROACH	
ADVANTAGES	DISADVANTAGES
1 Avoids open conflict	1 Delays the resolution
2 Gives time for better solution	2 Requires parties to set aside goals
3 Gives time for parties to get to know each other	3 Creates an uneasy truce with conflict just below the surface
4 Reduces short-term hurt	4 Results in a displacement of the conflict with the energy going into solving trivial difficulties
5 Imposes restraints on both parties	5 Produces 'traitors' and scapegoats

THE DEFENSIVE APPROACH

Passive resistance such as was used by Ghandi and his followers against British rule in India is often the only reasonable approach when one party is stronger in power or position, but the weaker is determined to pursue its goals whatever the cost. A defensive stance in a conflict is usually the signal for a long encounter. The defender will have to withstand sustained and wearing attacks.

The M62 motorway in northern England links the east and the west of the country across the Pennine hills. It is Britain's highest motorway. Construction of the road was delayed considerably by the presence of a farmhouse which lay directly in the path of the highway. For months the authorities sought to move the tenant. Construction workers added their own pressures with noise and light twenty-four hours a day, but still the owner sat tight. Eventually, to avoid further delay, the road was rerouted and today the farmhouse still stands — occupied — *between* the east- and west-bound carriageways! The strengths and weaknesses of the defensive approach are set out in the following table.

THE DEFENSIVE APPROACH	
ADVANTAGES	DISADVANTAGES
1 Separates the parties	1 Protracted conflict likely
2 Gives time for resolution	2 Delays resolution
3 Protects the weak	3 High social/ psychological costs
4 Avoids open conflict	4 Initiative always with attacking party
5 Reduces damage initially	5 Increased bitterness

THE OFFENSIVE APPROACH

When threatened or faced with conflict, 'The best method of defence is attack' is a view that is widely held. 'Do unto others before they do it unto you!' Resist aggressively.

For years Iran and Iraq have been in dispute over ownership of the Shatt Al Arab waterway that separates their countries near the Gulf of Persia. In 1980 it was in Iranian hands. Then, on 22 September of that year, the Iraquis launched a surprise attack on Iran, hoping for a quick victory. At the time of writing, the war is in its eighth year. As the table below shows, taking the offensive has its positive side too.

THE OFFENSIVE APPROACH	
ADVANTAGES	DISADVANTAGES
1 Shows you mean business	1 Leads to escalation
2 Has the element of surprise	2 Risk of early defeat
3 Tests the strength of the opposition	3 Difficult to control
4 Gives you an opportunity to test your own strength	4 Exposes your position and intentions
5 Often catches the opposition off guard	5 Inflicts maximum damage on all parties

THE CONFRONTATIONAL APPROACH

Confrontation is a much maligned word. We use it synonomously with 'conflict', failing to realise that conflict is a state and confrontation is an approach to that state.

To confront requires us to face and work with the opposition. It requires us to:

—Get close
—Say 'This is where we are'
—Say 'This is where I see you'
—Say 'We cannot go on like this. Something has to change, and has to change now'
—Be committed to a solution
—Work hard to resolve the conflict.

Confrontation is also aggressive—it is an attempt to force our desire for a solution on to the other party, whether it is ready or not. Nevertheless, confrontation does value peace. In October 1962 the superpowers came close to all-out war when the USSR began to install missile bases in Cuba. President John F Kennedy ordered American naval vessels to intercept and search Russian ships and to prevent their access to Cuba. The high-risk strategy was based on the assumption that the best way to prevent war was to confront the enemy. Although in this instance it was successful, such confrontation can result in a significant escalation of conflict.

THE CONFRONTATIONAL APPROACH	
ADVANTAGES	DISADVANTAGES
1 Forces parties together	1 Often misread
2 Precipitates developments—good or bad	2 May result in an escalation of the conflict
3 Usually results in a clarifying of the issues	3 Timing is often wrong and one party is forced back into defence or is encouraged to go on to the offensive
4 Demonstrates commitment to peace but not at any price	4 Results in a one-sided initiative and is often seen as threatening
5 Relies on words and action	5 High risk

Five More Options

Midway between co-operation and resistance lies 'non co-operation'—the work-to-rule approach: 'We will do only that which the law or the agreement or your power requires us to do and no more.' Similarly, midway between aggression and passivity is assertion—willingness to state our case clearly and strongly without denying the rights of the other party. Note the difference between aggression and assertion. Perhaps a few definitions would help us here.

Confrontation is used to describe a face-to-face encounter in a conflict. Thus it is possible to have a conflict without confrontation, but it is not possible to have a confrontation without a conflict.

Aggression is the term used to describe behaviour which seeks to harm the opposition. It need not be unprovoked, but is designed to force the wishes of one party on another at the expense of the other's interests, values or aims. Aggression is not helpful as a long-term strategy, though it may be necessary to precipitate a confrontation.

Assertion describes behaviour in which one party clearly states its interest, wishes, values or aims in such a way that others may hear and take account of the position and interest of the person who asserts. Assertiveness also encourages the other party to state its interest and aims — on the basis that reconciliation can only happen when people communicate openly and clearly.

These definitions show that confrontation and assertion may be helpful in the process of resolving conflict. Aggression may lead to resolution, but it rarely leads to reconciliation. We can now develop a table of options covering the full range of possible approaches to conflict. The table is based on our attitudes to our own goals and our attitudes to others' goals.

ATTITUDES TO OTHERS' GOALS

		CO-OPERATIVE	NON-COOPERATIVE	RESISTANT
A T T I T U D E S T O O W N G O A L S	PASSIVE	collaborate 1	avoid 2	defend 3
	ASSERTIVE	reconcile 4	compromise 5	negotiate 6
	AGGRESSIVE	confront 7	compete 8	attack 9

Nine Approaches to Conflict

Thus the five new options are to:

—Avoid
—Compromise
—Compete
—Negotiate, and
—Reconcile.

THE AVOIDANCE APPROACH—
PASSIVE NON-COOPERATION

It is possible to ignore the conflict and to keep as far away from the opposition as possible. For some of us, an uneasy truce is better than any other approach. Peace at any price is better than the cost of any conflict. We must remember, however, that avoidance does not remove the source of or the potential for conflict; it simply removes the opportunity. Avoidance is a case of 'Peace! Peace!' when there is no peace; but avoidance is a useful strategy when we are not ready to engage the opposition or when we don't believe the issues are worth fighting over.

THE COMPROMISE APPROACH—
ASSERTIVE NON-COOPERATION

At the core of the matrix of approaches to conflict is 'compromise'. It is probably the most widely used method of resolving differences. Each party is required to give a bit in order to accommodate the aims and targets of the other. Compromise assumes that:

—Each party is right and
—Each party is wrong and
—Each party is equal and
—Each party is honest and
—Each party is trustworthy and
—Each party will abide by the rules.

Because these assumptions are rarely correct, compromise rarely results in an effective resolution. Both parties usually feel equally bad about the solution! This feeling arises from the fact that in a compromise nobody wins; it is in effect a lose/lose outcome.

THE COMPETITIVE APPROACH—
AGGRESSIVE NON-COOPERATION

'May the best man win' is the term which accurately characterises a competitive approach to conflict. For competition
to work, the aims of the parties must be similar but mutually
exclusive; as for athletes in a race, only one can win.

Auctions offer another competitive model; only the
highest bidder wins. Competitive approaches to the resolution of conflict often relate to promotion and position.
Since only one can be judged best, opportunity is given to
the competitors to show their mettle. Situations may even
be engineered to provide the chance for the competitors to
get to grips with each other. To work, a competitive
approach requires clear rules and a strong referee. Uncontrolled competition can result in significant hurt for the
opponents—and in some cases the spectators!

THE NEGOTIATIVE APPROACH—
ASSERTIVE RESISTANCE

Negotiation requires us to resist the aims of the opposition
and to assert our own aims strongly. The hard negotiator
will attempt to win as much as possible at the expense of
the other side. Whether this negotiation has to do with
management and unions, buyers and sellers, or groups
within a church or organisation, the issues are the same:

—How much can I gain?
—How little can I give away?

The answer to these questions will depend on where the
power lies, who can threaten most, what sanctions are
applicable, and what are the risks of failure.

The negotiative approach is aggressive in its nature and
implies a win/lose mentality. But negotiation is a poor way
to resolve conflict, since in the end both parties are likely to
lose. A 'victory' for one side will establish a base of resentment that will ensure the tactics in the next round of negotiations will be a tougher version of previous approaches.
Industrial Britain in the seventies was a classic example of
the weakness of negotiation to resolve conflict on a permanent basis.

THE RECONCILIATION APPROACH— ASSERTIVE COOPERATION

Co-operation and assertion are needed for reconciliation. Later we will examine reconciliation in detail. At the moment it is sufficient to say that reconciliation is no easy option; it is not a position of weakness, but one of strength. It does not require us to give up what we are or what we aim for; rather, it requires us to assert what we are and what we want. 'God was reconciling the world to himself in Christ.'[6] That was no easy way out; that was no yielding of values; that was no compromise.

As we have seen, each approach has its own merits, yet only assertive co-operation is likely to yield the unity of mind which is peace. The other eight approaches may have their time and their place, but what our society needs now is not more avoidance, more compromise or more competition: what we need now is more reconciliation—fewer sword-bearers and more peacemakers. Which are we?

Return now to your scores in the table on page 69 and check your own approach. Now enter your scores in the nine boxes below. Total your scores both across and down the matrix to give you subtotals A to F.

1 COLLABORATOR ———	2 AVOIDER ———	3 DEFENDER ———	A ——— (1+2+3)
4 RECONCILER ———	5 COMPROMISER ———	6 NEGOTIATOR ———	B ——— (4+5+6)
7 CONFRONTER ———	8 COMPETITOR ———	9 ATTACKER ———	C ——— (7+8+9)

D ——— (1+4+7)	E ——— (2+5+8)	F ——— (3+6+9)

INTERPRETATION OF RESULTS

Again, your total score should be 45. The maximum for any one of the nine approaches is 10, the minimum 0. If you have scored 7 or more for any one approach, then that approach is one you 'prefer'. Approaches for which you scored 3 or less are those you tend to avoid. If you scored more than 20 points in any of the subtotals A to F, then check the following points.

Subtotal A. If you have a high score in this set, more than 20, you are being too passive in conflicts. Such little assertion may cause you to withdraw when faced with even slight opposition. It is difficult to operate as a peacemaker unless you have a high commitment to peace and are prepared to put yourself at risk for the sake of your commitment. In Chapter Five the issue of assertiveness/non-assertiveness is explored.

Subtotal B. Those with a high score in this area will tend to be articulate, influential and have success in peacemaking activities. Although compromise and negotiation can bring about agreement, the decision to pursue them should be undertaken guardedly, for at best they bring only temporary agreement. Also, non-cooperative and resistant elements could lead you to be somewhat inflexible and dogmatic in your approaches to conflict (see Chapter Seven). Paying more attention to listening and understanding where the parties are, rather than concentrating on where you want them to be, will help your effectiveness.

Subtotal C. A high score here should be taken as a warning light. Your approach may be too aggressive and self-centred. Although confrontation helps sometimes, competition and direct attacks do not further the cause of reconciliation. In acting as a peacemaker you should remember that you cannot, of course, force people into harmonious relationships: instead, reconciliation comes about when the parties share common goals, when there is creative thinking, not coercion (see Chapter Six).

Subtotal D. This is the co-operative domain. Your ability to work with others is high, although you are not afraid to speak your mind or to challenge wrong behaviour. If, however, you have a score of more than 20 here, as well as a high score on subtotal A, your concern for your own needs may actually prevent you working through difficult, long-standing conflicts.

Subtotal E. A high score here characterises non-cooperative behaviour—unhelpful in peacemaking. This often results from an overly strong concern for your own goals and belief in the rightness of your position. Thus when you come to help others resolve their differences, you will be strongly tempted to take sides and so sacrifice impartiality. (Chapter Nine will offer some techniques for increasing co-operative behaviour.)

Subtotal F. If you scored more than 20 here, you are resisting circumstances. Such behaviour may prevent you from getting what you *don't* want, but it rarely gets you what you really *do* want. You will probably not agree with me when I say that you will face great difficulties as a peacemaker (now don't get all defensive again!). Your strong ability to resist pressure would, however, be of value in some conflicts where one party is very much more powerful than the other; in such a case your capacity to withstand pressure could ensure an equitable solution for all.

An ideal sum of high scores for a would-be peacemaker is B plus D, since this combination leads to *assertive co-operation*, the classic reconciliation behaviour. The remainder of this book will concentrate on the development of this approach.

Summary

I have attempted to show that the sword-bearers are in the ascendancy today; further, that there have always been more sword-bearers than peacemakers. This is the reality with which the peacemaker has to deal. As the ploughman faces the fallow field it is not barren; the ground has yielded the weeds and thistles which must be rooted out, turned over and destroyed before a new planting can begin. The ploughman knows his soil, he knows the weed. So, too, the peacemaker needs to know the nature and form of the conflicts he or she will face. This, then, has been our initial aim: to describe the nature of conflict.

I have set out the history of conflict in the world and the major processes by which conflicts grow. We have considered the roots and shoots of conflict and considered how best to deal with them. We have examined the nine major approaches to conflict and the options open to us, only one—reconciliation—offers any lasting solution. Yet since the sword-bearers seem to be destined to continue their ascendancy, even our successes as peacemakers will be short-lived. But even short-lived successes are worth having. Remember: 'There can be no more important matter for the future of the world than conflict resolution.'[7]

CHAPTER FIVE

THE MEANING OF RECONCILIATION

Temporary solutions are often the best we can achieve. In every state of concord lies the seed of future conflict. In every state of conflict the crucial elements for creating peace are hidden. The normal rhythm of life is concord-conflict-concord-conflict-concord. Thus all solutions are temporary.[1]

HAVING COME TO GRIPS with conflict, we can now turn our attention to peacemaking. The focus of the next few chapters is reconciliation without the intervention of a third party or mediator. The use of a peacemaker will be considered subsequently, as will the various methods that can be used to bring parties together. For the moment, then, we shall focus on the process of peacemaking. We cannot build a steam engine unless we understand the processes of energy conversion; we cannot build a nuclear reactor unless we understand the processes of nuclear fission. So too with peace; we cannot build it unless we understand the processes of reconciliation.

In the next few chapters we shall therefore examine what is meant by reconciliation. How does it differ from negotiation, or from compromise? What are its key features, and what steps are necessary in order to achieve it? In Chapter Six, we shall examine the tactics of peacemaking, what approaches to use and when. In particular we shall look at some of the skills and attributes needed for peacemaking. In Chapters Seven and Eight we shall examine the critical first step in conflict resolution — taking the initiative — and we shall discover why it is that so many peace overtures are aborted and simply lead to more conflict.

No change takes place without a price; this is true also of the reconciliation process. What is the price? Who pays it? How can it — or should it — be minimised? These are the questions addressed in Chapter Nine. In Chapter Ten, we shall then think through the role of the peacekeeper. Once peace has been re-established, how can we prevent it from breaking down?

You will probably find this section of the book the most challenging, for now we must look inwards — or at least in the mirror. What we see there may not encourage us too much; but we can take heart: it is only what we are *now* that we see. We can change if we are prepared to pay the price. The beauty of reconciliation is that although the cost is high, the cost is also shared.

Assertiveness

One reason there is so little peace is that we use the wrong processes to try to settle the differences between us. In the last chapter we saw that reconciliation may be defined as *assertive co-operation*. We now need to understand more fully the nature of assertion. It is also valuable to understand the differences between *mediation, arbitration, negotiation, conciliation* and *reconciliation*: words commonly used and commonly misunderstood. Each of these processes is widely used today to try to settle disputes. Their success rate is not high, but when we remember that the natural outcome of conflict is more conflict, then we should be prepared to use and support any process that genuinely seeks settlements.

We used the words 'assertion' and 'aggression' in Chapter Four in relation to our attitude to our own goals (page 76). 'Assertion' describes our behaviour when we seek to achieve or express our own needs, opinions, feelings and beliefs in a direct, open and honest way and at the same time seek to encourage the reciprocal expression by the other party. We recognise that we have rights to be met, and that those around us also have rights we should be seeking to ensure are met. Assertion recognises that we *are* our brothers' keepers. We all have rights. We have rights that come from the laws of the land; we have rights that come from the policies and practices of the organisations in which we work and serve; we have rights that come from our human identity—in the fact that we are made in the image of the infinite God. Ken and Kate Back describe assertiveness this way:

So assertiveness is based on the beliefs that in any solution:

—You have needs to be met
—The other people involved have needs to be met
—You have rights; so do others
—You have something to contribute; so do others.

The aim of assertive behaviour is to satisfy the needs and wants of both parties involved in the situation.[2]

Unfortunately, 'assertion' has certain negative undertones in present English usage. It conjures up an image of a pushy, aggressive person. This is particularly so in the USA, where assertion has been favoured by the women's liberation movement and misrepresented in the media. However, assertion is a positive, helpful behaviour when it comes to the resolution of conflict, and it is essential in the process of reconciliation.

AGGRESSION

Assertion should not be confused with aggression, which seeks to ignore the rights of others and ignore or dismiss the needs, wants, opinions and feelings of other parties. Aggression is basically selfish and puts other people second; assertiveness, on the other hand, sees all as being equal. As we shall see, to be assertive is to 'love your neighbour as yourself'—the second great commandment.[3] Such concern for self and others is true assertion. By asserting myself and helping others do the same, I am affirming their rights; I am affirming their differences without diminishing self. On the other hand, aggression diminishes my brothers and sisters. It seeks to undermine and devalue their positions and beliefs. Even when I am right, it is dangerous to impose my rightness on others; the outcome is rarely an improved relationship. We discover that aggression not only diminishes my brothers and sisters; it diminishes me.

NON-ASSERTION

An alternative approach to your own and others' needs is non-assertion. Failure to express my needs, opinions, feelings and beliefs, or expressing them in an apologetic, self-effacing manner in order to please others and avoid conflict is termed 'non-assertion'. When I say 'yes' when I really want to say 'no', or 'no' when I really want to say 'yes', I am being non-assertive. I may feel threatened, isolated, at risk, unworthy and of no consequence, so I go along with the crowd; I agree to let the other party dominate the situation and my own needs. Non-assertion may avoid outward conflict, but it does not avoid conflict, for it simply pushes the conflict underground where it becomes an inner conflict—unresolvable until I come to face the unreasonable demands of others and learn to assert myself as someone with value to myself and others. Both aggression and non-assertion may have their roots in low self-esteem (see page 52).

Can you recognise the different behaviours? Here are a few examples. Read them and see if you can correctly identify them. You will find a suggested answer list at the end of this chapter, page 88. Are the following statements assertive, non-assertive or aggressive?

1 'What I want to see is more participation.'
2 'I would prefer to go to Paris.'   '
3 'Forgive me for asking but I thought, well, you know, that we had agreed to go to Paris.'
4 'You know what happened the last time we agreed to go where you had suggested.'
5 'Everyone knows that won't work. Why are you so blind?'
6 'I could not finish that before 5 pm.'
7 'I'd watch my step if I were you.'
8 'It's only my view, and of course I might be wrong.'

9 'What on earth were you trying to do?'
10 'From my experience I could not agree with that.'
11 'Well, I'm not sure, perhaps er....'
12 'I really must get round to writing to Mary soon.'
13 'John, I did not receive your report on time.'
14 'You're always saying things like that.'
15 'I need more time to think about this.'
16 'I'm terribly sorry. I didn't mean to question your judgement.'
17 'That's just typical of you.'
18 'I must apologise for the presentation—I'm not very good at these things.'
19 'Oh, don't worry about what I think. It's not important.'
20 'I'm getting frustrated by all this talk and no action.'

It should be noted that non-verbal communication (body language) and the context of the words can alter their impact. Our behaviour is more than our words. Assertion will show itself in our tone of voice, in our inflections, in all our non-verbal behaviour. Are you aware of the messages that you give? Reconciliation has to do with the rebuilding of relationships—a true meeting of minds and hearts. Such a meeting recognises the value of assertiveness, for without it there will only be a meeting of masks.

In addition to the assertive attitudes described above, page 86, there are certain key features of reconciliation that distinguish it from other peacemaking approaches such as mediation, arbitration and negotiation. Before we can identify these, it will be useful to establish some of the differences between the various approaches to peacemaking.

Mediation

Mediation involves a *third party*. Unable or unwilling to resolve their differences, they call in a third person, who intervenes in the process and seeks to help solve the conflict between the parties. I shall examine this approach towards the end of *Peacing Together*, but at the moment it is sufficient to note that mediation involves an independent party as a go-between. The mediator may become involved as a result of a request from one or both of the parties, or the mediator may take the initiative and offer to be involved in attempting to restore peace. However the involvement comes about, a mediator will have to:

— Be acceptable to both parties
— Have authority with both parties
— Be seen to be acting wisely and responsibly
— Be detached and objective
— Understand the positions and feelings of both sides
— Be skilled in the process of problem-solving
— Have a high degree of interpersonal skills.

If one or both of the parties detect that the mediator is flawed, the process may break down.

Mediation is concerned to bring parties from their extreme positions to a middle ground acceptable to both. The mediation process may be protracted, with many shufflings back and forth, before face-to-face talks take place and final agreement is reached. The success or failure lies in the social skills of the mediator. This is very different from arbitration.

Arbitration

Arbitration is concerned with *judging between the position of two parties*. It does not necessarily imply or seek reconciliation or middle ground. The arbitrator's task is to understand the position of both sides and to propose a 'fair' solution. The solution proposed may be binding on the parties, depending on the terms agreed for arbitration. The parties are not guaranteed satisfaction at the hands of the arbitrator, nor is reconciliation an aim of the process.

In the case of management and unions, the result may be a temporary but wary peace— until the next round of negotiations. Or one party may refuse to accept the judgement of the arbitrator and seek to increase the conflict.

Arbitration is the main method of settling disputes in tribal systems where the 'elders' listen and judge in disputes, but there the judgement is usually binding. In St Matthew's Gospel a process of arbitration is described for use within the context of the church. In the book *Restoring Fellowship*, the authors say of this biblical process: 'The formula is not offered with a guarantee. But if followed correctly, the offended has peace of mind in his assurance that he has done his best.'[4]

However, arbitration is often the only course, although it might be 'worse than robbery'—as Gavin Kennedy describes in his book *Everything Is Negotiable*. He illustrates the dangers of arbitration by reference to a nationalisation deal in Britain in the 1970s. The British warship builders, Yarrows, were nationalised in 1977 and for several years fought hard for what they considered to be a just compensation.

Yarrows valued their shipbuilding assets at £16 million, and the British government valued them at £6 million (at least that was the total compensation offered). Two other formerly independent companies contested the amounts of compensation they were awarded. However, one of the former yards settled with the government—under protest —and a week later Yarrows followed suit. They had been disappointed that the new Conservative government did not endorse their fight against the previous Labour government's nationalisation formula. They were also advised that the only recourse open to them was to go to arbitration. If they did so, they were told, 'there is no assurance that any award made would be any better than they had now, and there is always the risk that it might be worse.'[5] Faced with that as an alternative, Yarrows decided to settle for what they could get.

Arbitration is not assertive, since we are required to surrender our rights and needs to the judgement of a third party. Arbitration is often a lose/lose process, at the end of which the parties may be no closer together.

Negotiation

Negotiation is basically a power game. It does not lead to reconciliation; it leads to *a win for the most able, skilful or powerful* party. Information is ammunition in negotiations —if you know the other party's needs and weaknesses, you can exploit them to achieve your own goals. The emphasis is on 'me first, others next'. We really don't care who comes second. The more power we have, the more aggressive we can be and the greater the threats we can offer. Negotiation is a win/lose game, which in the long-term relationship is a lose/lose outcome, for no matter who wins, the relationship suffers.

Recognising the negative side-effects of hard bargaining and the problems of non-assertion, a number of specialists in the field of negotiation have searched for new approaches. In their book *Getting to Yes*,[6] the authors propose a joint problem-solving approach as a more effective process in which both parties agree to own the problem rather than blame each other for the problem. As we shall see, this is crucial to the act of reconciliation.

Conciliation

Conciliation assumes that reconciliation is not possible and that the best that can be achieved is *a minimising of the damage to the conflicting parties*. Conciliation services are booming on both sides of the Atlantic as marriage break-down increases and management/union divides widen. Traditionally, third parties are hired to get the best deal possible in financial and resource terms, but the social, economic and psychological damage is often too high. A new breed of advisor has therefore emerged midway between a negotiator and an arbitrator. The task of the conciliator is to bring the parties to agreement with a minimum of damage. The assumption is that the role of the conciliator is based on a mutual agreement not to agree. The basic conflict between the parties will not be resolved. Only the secondary effects—such as 'Who gets what?'—will be dealt with.

In summary we can say that:

—Arbitration seeks fairness through judgement
—Mediation seeks common ground
—Negotiation hopes for one winner
—Conciliation assumes two losers.

In all of these approaches assertion plays its part, but reconciliation is rarely the outcome. Nevertheless, a bad solution may be better than no solution, an enforced peace is better than open war, for at least it gives time for talk, time for better solution.

Reconciliation

We have defined reconciliation as 'assertive cc -operation'. This means that each party is expected to be himself and actively co-operate to find a solution. The Collins Dictionary defines reconciliation. as 'to become friendly after an estrangement'.

In the New Testament the word *katalassein* is translated 'to reconcile'. Its meaning in the Greek is 'to change thoroughly'. It is used to describe a thorough change in relationships between:

—mankind and God[7]
—all Creation and God[8]
—the world and God[9]
—husband and wife.[10]

In the King James version of the Bible other words are translated as 'reconciliation'. In relation to our subject, one is relevant: that pertaining to brother and brother.[11] The root word here is *dialloiesthai*, which means 'to be changed throughout'. Thus we see that reconciliation has at its centre the concept of relationships which are changed completely.

THOROUGHLY CHANGING RELATIONSHIPS

The thought that to reconcile means to change a relationship thoroughly gives us the key to the question of why so many peace initiatives fail. One answer is because they treat the position, not the people! Too much focus is on the positions adopted and not enough on the relationship. Most attempts to bring peace focus on the fact and not the feeling, but both need to be changed if reconciliation is to take place (see pages 103 and 104).

The Old and New Testaments give some other thoughts on conflict and reconciliation. Here are ten commandments for reconciliation. They have their origins in the Bible. Let us look at each for a moment.

1 *The initiative is ours.* So often we hear words such as 'Well, don't expect me to do anything. It's *his* fault!' People put the blame somewhere else. We all like to be thought of

as the injured party. We are in the right — *he* should take the initiative to put the relationship back together. The wisdom of Jesus suggests this is not correct. It is true that in St Matthew's Gospel Christ does instruct the disciples to sort out their conflicts quickly and to do that by taking the initiative if they are in the wrong.[12] Go to your brother (or sister) if you have wronged him (or her), if he or she has anything against you; take the initiative and sort it out.[13] But later in the same Gospel Christ instructs his disciples in an even harder way: if your brother acts against you; if it is your brother's fault that conflict has developed — do not wait until he comes and confesses. Instead, go to him immediately and seek to sort matters out.[14] Whoever is at fault, the one who seeks peace will take the initiative. This is a test for those who think they have a role in this kind of work. Do I regard the care and maintenance of my relationships with others as my own responsibility? The answer must be 'yes'.

2   *Act now.* A breakdown of relationships is viewed seriously in the Bible. Selfishness is the root of many evils, and as we have seen in Chapter Three, is the source of all conflicts. The longer a conflict remains unresolved, the greater the damage to the relationship. Conflict with others disturbs our inner peace and affects our relationship with our God[15] since it puts us in breach of the great commandment to love our neighbours as ourselves.[16] Many relationships have broken down and without reconciliation have passed feuds and vendettas from one generation to another.

The infamous massacre of Glencoe is a classic example. In 1692 a detachment of soldiers under the charge of Captain Robert Campbell arrived in the territory of the Clan McDonald with instructions to wipe out the clan for failing to sign on time an oath of allegiance to the Crown. Relationships between the two clans had never been easy, but the soldiers arrived in the depth of the Scottish winter, and the Clan McDonald gave them shelter and hospitality. The Campbells used this ancient law to their advantage and on the twelfth night of their stay with the McDonalds, at a prearranged signal, rose up in the darkness and slaughtered their hosts. The enormity of this treachery shocked the

Highlanders. To this day there is still animosity between the descendants of those who escaped the massacre and the Campbells.[17]

The gradual breakdown of the enlarged family has reduced the incidence of feuds, but in country areas and in towns and churches where mobility is still low, it is not uncommon for conflicts to last for generations. The isolated families of Hatfields and McCoys in the Appalachian mountains are legendary in America for such lasting conflict. Disputes between the two families go back many generations.

3 *Keep our own peace.* We saw in Chapter Three some of the offshoots of conflict: anxiety, depression, etc. These are potentially more harmful than the conflict itself. As Jesus prepared to face his greatest conflict, he was careful to stress to his followers that it is possible to be surrounded with hostility and yet be at peace with myself and God.[18] This is one secret of paying the cost of bringing about a reconciliation, as we shall see later in Chapter Ten of *Peacing Together*.

4 *Share our peace.* An ancient Christian sect was known as the Stylites. Followers of this cult sought to find their peace in isolation, but not in remoteness. To achieve their goals, the Stylites built pillars and sat on top of them, fed and watered by their faithful. Their most famous disciple was Simon Stylites, who is reputed to have sat at the top of his forty-foot pillar for sixty years![19]

It is not sufficient simply to experience our own inner peace; as peacemakers we must have a desire to communicate that peace to others. St Paul reminds the church at Corinth that it has experienced reconciliation and should therefore share it with society.[20]

This mission of 'peacing'—bringing peace into society —seems to be all but lost to many sections of the church today. Christians have become more associated with internal division than external peacemaking. The squabbles go on among some Anglicans as to the wisdom of ordaining women; among some Catholics as to a proper understanding of birth control; among some Baptists and Brethen as to the extent to which Christians should be separate from 'the

world'; among house churches as to the meaning of authority; and among almost all churches as to the proper use of
the 'sensational' charismatic gifts of healing, tongues, and
prophetic utterance. It is of course true that conflict is good
news material whereas peace is viewed as tame and unat-
tractive. But 'peacing' must become the stuff that news is
made of.

5 *Confess our part*. Conflict hurts—both parties. There are
no 'uninjured parties' in conflict. Both sides therefore need
individual healing, in addition to the healing of the relationship: healing from anger, resentment and fear. During
the process of reconciliation, each party needs to experience
an inner reconciliation, to God and to self. Each needs to
experience an inner healing. When we are dealing with
inner conflict, the 'parties' are parts of our personality and
being. These parts have been variously described as:

—id, ego, super-ego (Freud)
—old man, new man (Scripture)
—the flesh and the spirit (Scripture)
—*animus* and *anima* (Jung).

One writer described all too well the familiar struggle
between what we want or know we ought to want to
do—and what we actually do: 'When I want to do good,
evil is right there with me.... What a wretched man I am!
Who will rescue me from this body of death?'[21]
   The power of guilt—real or false—to destroy the whole
personality is well known, and so is the remedy—confession. To say 'I am wrong'; to say 'I should not have done
this'—to *confess*—is a first step in the healing process.
Bring the dark things into the light and declare the dark
side to be part of you rather than part of the other person. In
conflict we are at fault, so we start there and confess our
part (see also pages 106 and 107).

6 *Renounce conflict*. Reconciliation does not follow from
confession—it follows from repentance. Such was the
declaration of St John the Baptist, Christ and the apostles:
'Repent and be baptised, every one of you, in the name of
Jesus Christ so that your sins may be forgiven.'[22] The
biblical basis for all reconciliation is repentance—a fact

often overlooked. We are not asked to forgive if there is no repentance. In St Luke's Gospel Christ describes the process of forgiveness: 'If your brother sins, rebuke him, and if he repents, forgive him. If he sins against you seven times in a day, and seven times comes back to you and says, "I repent," forgive him.'[23] Note the principles here:

—There is a recognition of the problem (sin)
—There is a recognition of a real relationship based on love (brother)
—There is open confrontation of the problem (rebuke)
—Forgiveness is conditional (if)
—Repentance is the key to forgiveness (repents)
—Forgiveness follows on repentance automatically
—Forgiveness is not conditional on your expectations but only on the other's attitude of repentance
—Forgiveness is not conditional on the likelihood of future failure, only on the person's present attitude!

Without repentance, no thorough change is possible; the inner reconciliation comes from repentance, not simply confession. But reconciliation cannot come without confession, either. The statement 'Well, whatever I did, I'm sorry' is no basis for repentance or reconciliation. Repentance requires us to recognise our failings, to face them, to confess them and to turn from them. Only then can we be forgiven; only then can we forgive; only then can the relationship be thoroughly changed.

7   *Forgive those who act against us.* Forgiveness is a three-way process; it involves God's attitude to me, my attitude to others and my attitude to myself. First, all conflict has its roots in selfishness and as such puts self before God. We cannot experience inner wholeness—a thoroughly changed conscience—without knowing God's forgiveness: 'Forgive us our debts, as we also have forgiven our debtors.'[24] Inner healing begins with knowing God's forgiveness.

Inner reconciliation also requires us to forgive what has been done against us. As long as we continue to blame, accuse and resent, there can be no inner or outer reconciliation. Forgetting is not forgiveness, since forgetting can only come as a result of forgiveness. In his book *Caring Enough To Forgive*, David Augsburger says:

> When "forgiveness" denies that there is anger, acts as if it
> never happened, smiles as though it never hurt, fakes as
> though it's all forgotten—Don't offer it. Don't trust it. Don't
> depend on it. It's not forgiveness, it's magical fantasy.[25]

To forgive, we must be prepared to face the past, recognise
the hurt, commit ourself to a new relationship and attitude
and face the future with hope.

Inner reconciliation further requires us to be able to
forgive ourselves on the basis that God has forgiven us for
Christ's sake and that we have given genuine forgiveness
to others. Without self-forgiveness we are denied inner
peace, since guilt will continue to disturb and shatter us.
We cannot be reconciled to others if we are not reconciled
to God and to self. Reconciliation begins in us. When we
have experienced it inwardly we can begin to experience it
in our relationships.

8 *Keep the conflict contained.* We have seen the dangers of
allowing conflicts to run out of control. When conflict does
arise, it can be contained by sticking to the issues which
have given rise to the difference and by keeping the conflict
limited to the original parties. As a child I still recall the fear
that came from discovering I had got myself into a fight
with someone whose brother was in the army and would
come and 'bomb your street!'. My brothers were not old
enough to be in the army, navy or airforce, so I felt very
vulnerable! It is a temptation to pull in support from as
many quarters as possible when we are threatened. This
enlargement of the dispute makes the resolution of it all
that more difficult. Parents pull in their children; children
try to divide their parents; and mothers-in-law are carica-
tured as stealing the stage of most family feuds!

Another aspect of containment is confidentiality. There
is always the risk that a conflict shared is a conflict doubled.
The Book of Proverbs has many cautionary words to say
about the danger of indiscreet reporting—'Whoever
repeats the matter separates close friends.'[26]

9 *Listening.* The story is told of a famous flautist who
claimed that music—his music—could calm the most
troubled breast and bring warring parties to a state of

peace. In several public demonstrations he played to groups of people who were in conflict—husbands and wives, unions and management, etc—with significant success. His music seemed to reduce levels of anger and violence long enough for relationships to be re-established. His critics, however, claimed that it was all a confidence trick and that the parties had been briefed beforehand. In response, the flute player claimed that he could calm even the most ferocious and wild of animals. With sponsorship from the flute manufacturers, a test was set up in Africa by a water-hole where gazelle, elephants and lions were known to drink.

At dusk the flautist drew out his instrument and began to play. Haunting melodies filled the night air and soon the little creatures of the plains began to gather. Overcoming their fear they lay down in a circle around the musician. Soon the larger beasts—elephants, rhinos and giraffe—were forming a second circle, each beast at peace with its neighbour. Suddenly there was a roar as an old lion leapt from the back and, landing on the flautist, proceeded to tear him limb from limb.

'Stop! Stop!' chorused the animals.'

'We are listening to the music!'

'Pardon?' replied the deaf lion. 'You need to speak up, I can't hear very well!'

When it comes to peacemaking, some of us can't hear very well. We are used to the words of war; we are used to the sounds of violence; we are used to declaring our own rights and interests and so are deaf to the language of peace. *Peacing Together* came about as a title in part because the English language is not adequate for describing our needs. But even when language is adequate, we are prepared to give anyone our voice, but few our ears; anything rather than seek to understand the position and interests of others!

10 *Focus on our own faults.* There is rarely an innocent party in a conflict. So when we find ourselves in confrontation with others, we should look inwards. St Paul found himself having to write in a confrontational manner to the church at Corinth. It was his second letter, and things at the

city had deteriorated somewhat since he last wrote. How did he approach the delicate problem? He is open and directive, but he shares in the problem. It is his fault too that things are not right, so he takes part of the blame and expresses his own shame and concern that he has partly contributed to the problem.[27]

To recognise, then, that the dark side is always present in us and admit to our own failing is one way of reducing other people's defensiveness.[28]

Summary

Reconciliation is a state of unity rather than of peace. Peace still implies an emphasis on difference—'We are at peace with them'; whereas reconciliation implies an integration in which the 'we' and 'they' have been thoroughly changed to create 'us'.

Reconciliation requires the parties to be assertive. Mediation, arbitration and negotiation on the other hand normally involve non-assertion or aggression. The ten principles of reconciliation now place the responsibility for peace on us. This means we should always be seeking initiatives for peace.

ASSERTIVE, NON-ASSERTIVE OR AGGRESSIVE?

Bearing in mind the warnings on non-verbal and other influences in context, the statements on pages 86 and 87 can be classified as follows:

1	Assertive	11	Non-assertive
2	Assertive	12	Non-assertive
3	Non-assertive	13	Assertive
4	Aggressive	14	Aggressive
5	Aggressive	15	Assertive
6	Assertive	16	Non-assertive
7	Aggressive	17	Aggressive
8	Non-assertive	18	Non-assertive
9	Aggressive	19	Non-assertive
10	Assertive	20	Assertive

CHAPTER SIX

THE PRACTICE OF RECONCILIATION

Observers today are almost in unanimous agreement that our greatest need is for closer relationships. Demonstrating love for one another is our basic task. But love does not preclude conflict. Close relationships of love will only be possible when we learn to properly face conflict, rather than improperly avoiding it.[1]

FACED WITH CONFLICT, the easiest and surest way to approach it is to deal directly with the other party. Third-party involvement inevitably complicates matters, although if the conflict is in a phase three destructive condition, or even in the upper levels of phase two, then the involvement of a mediator is almost essential. In this chapter I want to focus on one-to-one reconciliation without the direct involvement of a third party.

As does conflict, so too reconciliation involves certain tactics that offer more likelihood of success than others. On reflection you will find that these are obvious and basic. Why then are they not more widely used? The reason must lie in our intentions; most of us would rather win than go to the trouble and the cost of being reconciled. This is a vital fact for the peace-seeker to bear in mind.

There are three phases to reconciliation, and they mirror the three phases in conflict escalation, which as we saw in Chapter Two are separation, divergence and destruction. For reconciliation to take place, the parties need to stop fighting, come together and re-establish their unity. The phases are therefore disengagement, convergence and integration.

Phase One — Disengagement

No reconciliation can take place until the fighting has stopped and the warring parties have disengaged. In inter-personal conflicts, the weapons too must be laid down and the violence, in whatever form, must be renounced by both sides. As long as the combatants remain locked in struggle, there can be no progress towards reconciliation.

Disengagement is a critical step because it involves high risk. Who will be first to refrain from striking a blow for 'victory'? Who will be first to say 'I can fight back, but I will not'? The party which first draws back from the conflict may find itself on the receiving end of an all-out assault as the opposition senses, wrongly perhaps, that the signals convey weakness and defeat, or at least that the other has run out of ammunition! Even when both sides agree to stop shooting and shouting, the risks that a stray bullet or com-ment will trigger the renewal of conflict are high. Thus the ceasefire must be reinforced by a truce.

Truce or Ceasefire?

A truce differs from a simple ceasefire in that it implies positive action—a search for agreement; whereas the ceasefire indicates only what we will not do. I will not react when I am provoked; I will not take advantage of your unguarded moments; I will not seek your harm and hurt at every—nor at any—opportunity. This is ceasefire. But also in a ceasefire I am on the alert, for the level of trust is low or non-existent. You are still my enemy, the future is still to be won and I have still my vision of victory. We still stand on the brink of violence.

A truce moves us one more step back from the brink. In the declaration of a truce we have both said, 'There can be no winners—at the moment.' More, we have declared that we are motivated to trust each other not to attack—at least in the short term. We are also willing to talk. Ceasefires are often arranged by third parties, which is one reason why they are so easily and readily broken; whereas the truce is usually the result of direct negotiation between the parties. In a truce, a temporary peace gives an opportunity to reduce further the potential for strife. It also gives the parties the opportunity to draw back from their positions of confrontation.

Rigid positions and attitudes contribute to strife. When people have fixed ideas; when dogma, doctrine and desire become absolute, immutable and 'truth', then the immovable becomes the unteachable, and the unteachable becomes the bigot, and the bigot will man any barricade in defence of his ignorance. Positions declare where we are now, but a truce declares that we would rather be somewhere else and gives both sides the chance to be flexible without loss of face in the eyes of the enemy or the watching world.

WITHDRAWAL

Withdrawal from confrontation is a major step towards lasting peace; entrenched positions are surrendered voluntarily; the troops are stood down; the battlefield is left undisputed. I give up the gains that I have achieved by force of arms. I say, 'It is not worth further suffering. It is not worth the cost of continued conflict.' Withdrawal is a significant signal that the cost of conflict is too high to go on paying.

Within the first phase of reconciliation we therefore see three steps: ceasefire, truce and withdrawal. Direct aggression has stopped; we no longer attack or compete with one another on sight, and we have stepped back from confrontation. We have backed off from pursuing our aims at any cost.

No longer do the committee meetings resound to our accusations and counter-accusations. For a while we will continue to look over our shoulders for the sign of surprise attacks — for trust is still low, and the peace is uneasy — but our unease only hurts *ourselves*. It no longer does damage to the opposition or those around. Progress has been made, but reconciliation is still some way off.

Phase Two—Convergence

Jane was twenty-three. She had left home at seventeen as a result of serious confrontations with her father. For those six years she had kept her distance from her parents—never visited them, only keeping in contact through Christmas cards and the occasional holiday postcard. Now her father was dying, and she felt guilty. Since she heard of his illness through a brief note in a birthday card from her mother, Jane had been in a state of confusion. She wanted to see her father again, but she was still afraid. Years of separation had not helped, for it was clear from her conversations that although she coped well on her own, inwardly she had been badly scarred by the conflict.

Over lunch one day she talked about her response to her mother's news. In the last three months she had written to her parents every week, and they had responded to each of her letters. Four weeks ago she had made the first phone call in six years and had phoned each Sunday afternoon since.

'Why are you sharing all this with me?' I asked. Jane worked in one of my departments, but I knew little of her personal situation.

'I want to know what I should do,' she explained.

I remained silent, but she went on and it all poured out: her regrets, her loneliness, her anger, her fear, her confusion; regrets that she had missed out on family life, 400 miles from home, and, as she saw it, unable to go home; the loneliness of the single girl in London; her anger at her father for bringing her to this point; her fear that he might die while she still felt as she did. She had expected that her letters—and now her phone calls—would make her feel better, but they didn't. They only seemed to emphasise the negative feelings that she had about herself, her situation and the six years of separation.

'Reconciliation is not a long-distance process,' I told her. 'It may begin that way, but eventually the parties need to meet, need to shake hands, to embrace one another, to feel and hear the touches and sounds of forgiveness.'

The story of the prodigal son[2] and the famous, yet ancient, account of the reconciliation of the twin brothers, Esau and

Jacob[3] illustrate graphically that reconciliation is about being together again, not only emotionally, but physically. Peacemaking is about bringing together, coming close, restoring and being with each other in a new relationship. Preparatory work may be needed, as in Jane's case, with letters and long-distance conversations, but the real peace comes when the one-time enemies stand together again.

Jane went back home the following weekend. Her father died just over four weeks later, but their peace had been made. 'As soon as our eyes met,' she told me later, 'it was as though everything was restored and healed!'

Jane's story illustrates convergence, phase two of reconciliation. Convergence is a process of coming together, of understanding the enemy—not that we may use the understanding to do the enemy harm, but that in understanding we may find common ground, common interests, and a desire for a common future and vision. 'Sharing' is a word I will often use during the remainder of this chapter, for without sharing there can be neither reconciliation, nor unity. Unfortunately this word has been devalued through overuse and misuse. But in the context of reconciliation, 'sharing' describes an intimate exchange of fact, feeling and hope. Most peacemaking processes, such as arbitration and negotiation, take into account only the first of these elements. There is no place for feelings in the majority of the approaches, so the focus is too much on the past and the present for the conciliators to be concerned about tomorrow. Of course tomorrow has no facts attached to it—only hopes, wishes and dreams, and these have no place in the logical basis of so many of our current reconciliation efforts.

SHARING THE FACTS

During conflict, the level of communication between parties falls off dramatically. Mistrust and suspicion cause us to look and listen for only those messages that confirm our stereotype of the enemy. The period of the conflict is therefore like a story-book with every second page missing or with the text impossibly blurred. The parties invent—

usually in the worst light—what they don't know about each other.

Communication needs to be re-established: we need to learn to listen again. That means spending time together talking: sharing where we are, what we did in the conflict and why, how we saw the other party and how we interpreted his action. Putting everything on the table in this way has a cleansing effect. It is also a critical step, for it may provide both parties with the opportunity to enter the conflict once again.

The prodigal son went home to share the facts with his father,[4] for no full reconciliation can take place merely on the basis of 'forget and forgive', as we shall see. J Grant Howard, in his book on interpersonal communication, concludes that 'Transparency is traumatic. Open communication is like getting an immunization shot. It hurts, but it helps. If you are looking for painless ways to grow toward each other and toward maturity, call off the search.'[5]

SHARING THE FEELINGS

But conflict is also about feelings, not just facts—about feeling afraid, different, alone and angry. It's about wrestling with feelings. Convergence brings the opportunity to come together physically and socially, but it must also bring the parties together emotionally and spiritually. This is the most difficult part of the convergence phase. We try to avoid talking about how we did feel and how we now feel because here we are at our most vulnerable; here we are most embarrassed. The temptation will be to say, 'It's OK. Forget it.' We should reject the temptation. We must share the feelings, or we will be left with unfinished business. David Augsburger explains: 'When "forgiveness" distorts feelings by denying that there was hurt, disconnecting from feelings of pain, squelching the emotions that rise, pretending that all is forgiven, forgotten, forgone—don't trust it.'[6]

As we shall see later in this chapter, page 106, the sharing is part of the cost of reconciliation, and we cannot avoid paying the cost.

SHARING THE VISION

Sharing the facts and the feelings will help parties come to terms with the past and the present, but the key issue now is whether they can get it together for tomorrow. What is needed is joint commitment to a very different future from that anticipated in a scenario of conflict. One future could be long-term avoidance—separation, divorce, emigration: 'You go your way and I'll go mine.' This would bring a degree of peace, but it is not the restoration of unity that reconciliation offers. The real prize of the convergence phase is a common vision—a joint future to which both parties give their commitment and energy.

For the parties in conflict, the convergence phase is complete when there is an agreed statement of intent—a vision—a clear statement of where they want the relationship to go and how they want the relationship to be in the future. With this before them, the parties are ready for the third phase in the reconciliation process.

Phase Three—Integration

The unity broken by the conflict—or the unity which never was but might have been—now lies between the parties as a joint goal, a target to be aimed at, a vision to be pursued. The peace that they hope for is not a one-time event to be celebrated at some point in the future. Rather, the peace is ongoing and will keep the two parties together in harmony and mutual support. Herein lies integration, in which each becomes his brother's keeper—owning and valuing the other's interests and well-being, recognising and appreciating each other's differences and seeking individual maturity. Integration heralds a thoroughly changed relationship that will hold the parties together in the face of the inevitable pressures to differentiate and begin once more the conflict. Integration implies a fusion of minds and wills; it is a melding of the spirits to create a new team spirit.

Reconciliation is rare in our society because integration is a profound, cathartic and spiritual process—of which most people are afraid. Even the words used to describe the three steps involved cause people to react defensively. Such defensiveness is a product of our surface, plastic, throw-away society—a society in which even relationships have become disposable.

Confession, repentance and forgiveness are the steps that lead to reconciliation. Old-fashioned words, yes; religious words, yes; but indispensable words if we want reconciliation. These words are missing from books on arbitration; they don't appear in the texts on negotiation; we don't find them in our search for excellence. Their absence accounts for the inadequacy of these three to bring about quality improvements in relationships, business, churches and families.

CONFESSION

In conflict both parties have acted wrongly, and both parties have been hurt. Both parties have also injured each other. Thus both parties need to confess.

A one-sided confession will not do. Augsburger says that reconciliation is 'a brother—brother, sister—sister process; a two-way mutual interaction of resolving differences and recreating relationships between persons of equal worth.'[7] Present peacemaking seeks to shield the parties from the consequence of their behaviour in conflict. When this happens, the gravity of conflict is diminished; the hurt is glossed over, and the bitterness and anger remain only to break out again. Clearly, there can be no reconciliation without confession.

To say we are wrong, to admit our part in the creation of the conflict is not easy. We lay ourselves open in confession. We are vulnerable, but that is not the main concern, which is to restore peace—not on the basis of surrender or submission, and not on the basis of ignoring the wrongs done, but in the hope of a new future.

Too many people are too ready to use St Paul's injunction to 'speak the truth in love'[8] as an excuse to say what they think is true about others, rather than in love and humility to state the truth about themselves. That is the only truth we will ever know first-hand. Reconciliation requires us to tell the world how we are—not how it is!

REPENTANCE

Confession takes us one step nearer peace. To admit our part is the first step in reconciliation, to repent of our part puts an end to our contributions to the conflict and opens the way to forgiveness, for there can be no forgiveness without repentance. Repentance requires us to say that we have been wrong; more, repentance requires us to say that we are sorry for our action and attitudes. And again more, repentance requires us to say we knew we were wrong—that indeed we acted selfishly and that, with help, we will not repeat that behaviour. Similarly if our enemy repents, then we are bound to forgive him![9]

FORGIVENESS

Faced with a repentant opponent we have no other option but to forgive. There is a cost, of course. With our forgiveness go our 'rights' to punish, take advantage and declare victory. Also with forgiveness comes the responsibility to accept, forget and begin anew—to 'change thoroughly' the relationship. And that means thoroughly changing our attitudes and behaviours, not simply requiring the other person to change. With forgiveness for the past and with what we intend for the future, reconciliation is now possible.

There is no assurance that conflict will finally end in this way. As we have seen, reconciliation is not inevitable in the short or long term; we cannot expect it; we must work at it and for it. Remember that the object of reconciliation is that the relationship may be changed thoroughly from discord to harmony; from conflict to peace; from hate to love. Reconciliation attempts to restore unity. It is an attempt to make one what has been divided.

The diagram following captures the three phases and nine steps in reconciliation. All nine are needed for unity to be restored.

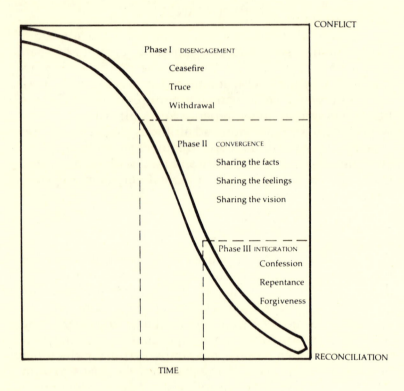

CONFLICT

Phase I DISENGAGEMENT

Ceasefire

Truce

Withdrawal

Phase II CONVERGENCE

Sharing the facts

Sharing the feelings

Sharing the vision

Phase III INTEGRATION

Confession

Repentance

Forgiveness

RECONCILIATION

TIME

The Reconciliation Curve

Making Reconciliation Work

Given that most conflicts do not end in reconciliation, we know that the process is not simple. We have already seen that 'confession', 'repentance' and 'forgiveness' are uncomfortable terms for twentieth-century people; in fact they seem more uncomfortable than 'hurt', 'fear' and 'guilt', and until we overcome our prejudices we will have little increase of peace among our societies. But even when we are prepared to run the real race of peace, there are still major barriers to be overcome. We will examine some of these in the next chapter.

To end this section on reconciliation I want to share with you three additional practices I have found to be indispensable in restoring relationships. These are immediacy, initiative and transparency.

IMMEDIACY

Jane's story, page 102, illustrates the importance of face-to-face contact in reconciliation, but her experience also highlights the need for a swift action to deal with conflict. For six years the separation from her father had blighted her life. Prolonged conflict can bring untold damage to the participants, and this is why immediate action is helpful in reconciliation. Do not wait. Act to restore the relationship *now*. Write that letter, make that call, set up that meeting. Yes, of course, there are risks involved; your advances may not be well received; you may be laying yourself open to more hurt; but these are only 'maybe's'. If you do not act, you can be certain you will be hurt. The need for swift action leads to the second indispensable practice in peace-making.

INITIATIVE

Fans of the Dr Seuss books and characters will be familiar with the Zax. Zax come in two varieties—the north-going Zax and the south-going Zax. One day two Zax met:

> Foot to foot. Face to face.
> 'Look here, now!' the North-going Zax said. 'I say!
> You're blocking my path. You're right in my way.
> I'm a North-going Zax and I always go north.
> Get out of my way, now, and let me go forth!'
>
> 'Who's in whose way?' snapped the South-going Zax.
> 'I always go south, making south-going tracks.
> So you're in MY way! And I ask you to move
> And let me go south in my south-going groove.'[10]

The Zax had been taught never to budge. Never to budge in the least: 'Not an inch to the west! Not an inch to the east!' With that kind of training neither could step aside, neither could take the initiative to resolve the problem and help both achieve their goals.

Who should take the initiative in reconciliation? Simply, the answer is 'I must!' But what if I am in the right? What if it is the other person who has wronged me? What if I am stronger and have the systems/policies/weapons and other people on my side? The answer is still, 'I must. All the more reason why I must!' Relatively speaking I have less to lose in making the gesture of holding out the olive branch. If I am strong, then I can seek peace out of my strength, not because I can threaten, but because this initiative is likely to be successful. St Paul is particularly insistent on this matter; it is the strong who make the allowances; it is the strong who should take the initiative.[11]

And what if I am in the wrong, or what if there are faults on both sides? Once again the answer is the same. If and when I become conscious of a developing conflict, then I must take action to restore the relationship and begin to move down that reconciliation curve.

Transparency

Initiative is one act associated with reconciliation that may correspond to an aspect of aggression (see page 85). It is therefore important that if I take an initiative to restore peace, I make my intentions very clear; otherwise my actions may be misinterpreted. This is the meaning of transparency.

Back in the early 1970s, a time of continuous industrial conflict in Britain, one company brought in an American managing director in an attempt to break the continuing cycle of management/union conflicts which had beset operations. He lasted four years, during which the level of confrontation and strikes increased. A month before he returned to the USA, the managing director invited all the shop stewards and conveners to a weekend retreat and final 'farewell'. There was deep suspicion until it emerged that no one else from the management was to be there—only the managing director and two dozen union representatives. The session began on Friday evening with a fine dinner and an explanation by the director of his purpose in calling the retreat.

According to the convenor who reported the event to me,

his speech was basically that he had come from the USA with great hopes of building bridges between management and unions and that for four years he had sought personally to get closer to the shop stewards and develop understanding, but he now had to admit failure. Before he went back to the States, he wanted to know why his advances had been rejected, what he could have done differently, and what if anything could be salvaged that might improve things in the future. Bob, the convener, recalled the reaction. 'We were all totally amazed,' he said. 'For the last four years we had seen the managing director as trying to undermine our solidarity, split us and pick us off one by one!' His intentions had been completely misread. In reply Bob had to ask the director, 'Why didn't you tell us what you were trying to do? You were certainly different from previous bosses, but we had no way of knowing what your aims were unless you told us!'

Transparency is essential. In front of any initiative must be the reason for it. Without this, any advances can so easily be misread as an attack. For a peace initiative brings the parties closer together physically; face-to-face you can see the colour of their eyes. Do you shoot or shake hands? Here is the point of confrontation. Your intentions must be crystal clear. That means you must be prepared to admit, 'We cannot go on meeting like this!'

Particularly with prolonged conflict, the barrier at this stage is one of trust. The Soviet Premier Gorbachev made a number of overtures to the West in 1987 in relation to nuclear arms reduction; however, the Reagan administration responded sceptically. The opposition was not to be trusted. In this mode the parties were at risk of locking each other into stereotypes. It has taken major shifts in behaviour through *perestroika* and *glasnost* to break the traditional image the West has of the Soviets. But mistrust continues, for example over missile verification procedures.

Thus, since reconciliation requires trust on both sides, we may have to make many transparent initiatives before the message gets across that we really do wish peace. If the relationship means more to us than our own pride, then we will persist with our gestures of peace. Having our pride dented is part of the price of reconciliation.

Summary

Reconciliation is more than a state of peace; it is a state of unity. The three main phases in reconciliation correspond to the three phases of conflict.

At the heart of reconciliation are confession, repentance and forgiveness. How do we feel about these words? If they make us uncomfortable; if they have embarrassing under- tones for us, then we must find other words which mean the same. We cannot bring about reconciliation without going through the steps implied by these three terms. It is the absence of confession, repentance and forgiveness which gives rise to so many ricocheting back and forth between conflict and peace. Peace comes too easily — kiss and make up; sign and shake hands, but don't look back. It's not necessary; forget it; it's over now. These are the sentiments that devalue peace. Peace is easy come, easy go. On the other hand reconciliation is a high-priced com- modity. The cost is confession, repentance and forgiveness. Who will start the bidding? The longer we wait, the higher the price.

CHAPTER SEVEN

THE BARRIERS TO RECONCILIATION

How often I have longed to gather your children together, as a hen gathers her chicks under her wings, but you were not willing.[1]

I N THIS CHAPTER I want to consider some of the barriers we face in our attempts to rebuild relationships. The barriers can be considered under two main categories — those of the environment in which the conflict has developed, and those that lie within us.

Environmental Barriers

Let us look first at some of the environmental blocks to reconciliation. The main barriers are in time, distance, lack of opportunity, public image and others' expectations.

TIME

There are two ways of looking at time and reconciliation; the first is to realise that reconciliation takes time. It is not a quick, cheap and nasty process, and it cannot be rushed. Some people's lives are so full or disorganised that they are unable to find time to rebuild their broken relationships. Time may also be used as an excuse—'I have no time.' What the person may mean is that it is not important enough for him to take time to work at reconciliation.

The second aspect of time concerns 'timeliness'. There is a time for every purpose—and 'there is a time for peace'.[2] In this sense, time presents a barrier related to the readiness of the parties to proceed. Although timeliness is a hindrance, it also can be used as the key to progress. By waiting for the time when the other party is ready we can avoid the reluctant reconciliation. Both parties must be ready and willing for the sharing of the cost. Reconciliation cannot be one-sided. We can use the methods described in Chapter Ten to bring the other party to the point of readiness—assuming of course that we too are ready!

DISTANCE

The prodigal son was in the far country when he decided that the time had come to go back home to his father.[3] Reconciliation is not a long-distance process; we may have to go a long way to achieve it. The bringing together is an intimate process and requires proximity. Distances are relative: we need not be a thousand miles from our adversary; we only need to keep avoiding him to create sufficient distance and prevent reconciliation getting under way. If we are seeking reconciliation, we should set up the meeting that will remove the distance. The story of Joseph and his brothers in the Old Testament demonstrates the need for the distance to be removed. Joseph had been sold as a slave by his jealous brothers. Years later they met again and Joseph set up a close encounter at which the reconciliation could take place.[4]

OPPORTUNITY

Joseph created the opportunity, not only by coming close to his brothers, but by making the reconciliation a private process. Servants were removed; the brothers' embarrassment, fear and confusion at the confrontation was hidden from all but Joseph. The pain of reconciliation is not for public consumption. The joy of restored unity should of course be shared widely, but repentance and confession are, in the context of interpersonal conflict, private processes.

In his book *Build That Bridge*, David Coffey describes processes in which public confession and repentance are involved for reconciliation. Where the reconciliation is required between one person and a large group, then a more open declaration of restoration is needed. Coffey describes a situation in which 'At the end of the meeting, for two hours, the church family stood in a single line so that each could embrace and encourage the leader and his wife and pledge his or her support in the difficult months that lay ahead.'[5] Clearly, where the conflict involves many people, all must be involved in the reconciliation, but that can hardly be described as 'public'. The amazing television confessions of some American evangelists in recent years should not be confused with reconciliation. That was not reconciliation; that was show business!

Beware also of the 'reconciliation' of obviously public conflict by private, secret processes which are 'confidential'. On such occasions many people have been aware of and probably drawn into the conflict, so the reconciliation too must be made public. This is part of the cost. It also helps prevent an early breakdown of the peace. (See also Chapter Ten.)

PUBLIC IMAGE

Often in a conflict one or both parties will protest innocence, placing the blame on the other party. As the conflict escalates into phase two (see page 41), so the need to build up the rightness of our case develops. This image building and destruction of the opposition's credibility makes subsequent confession and repentance difficult or impossible. It is only in realising that—apart from the original act which split the relationship—our own involvement in the escalation is in itself a cause for repentance and confession, that this barrier can thus be overcome.

I have been in situations in which reconciliation was desperately needed, yet to bring it about would have brought into the open attitudes and actions that would have embarrassed some of the more public leaders. Hence the relationship remained unrepaired in order that public credibility might be maintained. Converse circumstances create an equal problem. In recent years in UK politics the British people have seen the public disgrace of leading figures—for a token time thrust out into the cold, only to be brought back in at some opportune, yet to the public, undetermined time when for some reason, logic or process unknown, everything is OK again. This is not reconciliation, repentance or confession. This is politics!

EXPECTATIONS

Pressure exerted on the conflicting parties by colleagues, friends and relations can be a powerful incentive or disincentive to reconciliation. Consider this case.

We had known for some time that our friends' marriage was under pressure. We made frequent visits to them, and they visited us although we lived over 200 miles apart. Our friendship with them went back a long way to our college days, and they found our contacts with them supportive. We could help them clear the air, express feelings and make plans and commitments regarding the future conduct of their relationship. The marriage held together and began to settle down. Then the husband was made redundant— more pressure, more worry, more stress and more conflict. After a year of unemployment our friends decided to emigrate. Within nine months of leaving Britain they were separated and living separate lives. The removal of the constraints of others' expectations had allowed the conflict to increase until their marriage was destroyed.

Do not underestimate the power of others' expectations to keep peace.

The converse is also true. The expectations of others can sustain conflict and prevent reconciliation. This is particularly true when conflict has been sustained at the phase two level (see page 40) for protracted periods. The parties become stereotyped—locked into patterns of behaviour by those around who have come to expect continuing conflict. This attitude prevents any initiative towards reconciliation.

As it is, conflicting parties face so many *internal* barriers to reconciliation that it is essential for peace-seekers to break through these environmental constraints at an early stage. Overcoming the barriers will not be easy, and you may need help. If so, some of the strategies described later will help.

Internal Barriers

Since the major source of conflict is our own selfishness, then it follows that the major blocks to the resolution of conflict will also be internal. Let us consider the two most common inner barriers: fear and mistrust. Of course, the seeker of peace will encounter many others, especially those offshoots of selfishness described on page 56. But in many cases, the warring parties will simply not be aware of the reasons why they are unable to take initiatives towards the restoration of peace. They only experience the frustration and hurt that come from being locked into hostility. It is not, however, essential for the barriers to be recognised by the parties, provided a third party is able to reduce the barriers; thus reconciliation can move forward.

THE UNKNOWN

Faced with a conflict, most people are uncomfortable. Conflict represents a threat; it represents an undesirable and uncertain situation. That uncertainty triggers a series of reactions which create a powerful barrier to open behaviour. What will the opposition do? How far will he go? These two questions take us into unknown territory and increase our discomfort. Faced with the unknown, we tend to interpret the situation in the light of our own experience. When was the last time I was in conflict? What happened then? What does this situation mean for me now? If successful outcomes have been my experience of past conflicts, I will be encouraged and may adopt the same behaviour which resulted in the previous success. On the other hand if I have been badly hurt by previous encounters, I will tend to protect myself by whatever means I can, and my defensiveness will cause loss of opportunities for reconciliation.

MISTRUST

Reconciliation initiatives often break down because one or both parties lack the skill to handle the process. We shall examine the necessary skills in depth later, but we will look first at the skill of information handling. Reconciliation is an opening up process; it requires people to declare where they are and what they want. (This is *assertiveness*, see pages 84–87. It also involves a sharing of hopes, fears and feelings. Inevitably, this sharing of information places the parties at risk, for they now have data about each other they can misuse. Confessions can be broadcast, sold to the Sunday newspapers, or simply gossiped around the office or church. A high degree of vulnerability is incurred as a result. The mediator too, if one is involved, will become party to confidential information: how will it be handled? Can the mediator be trusted? Who will the mediator discuss it with? Can those people be trusted? Such questions increase our sense of vulnerability.

Information is also power and therefore may be used to intensify the conflict. But reconciliation cannot take place without discussion. Hence my lack of trust of the other party becomes a major barrier to restoring peace.

What, then, are some of the most common approaches taken to overcome these many barriers to reconciliation? Certainly not all of them are helpful!

Approaches

It is only too easy to let our own personalities intrude into the reconciliation process. We all have particular traits, and some of these can come between ourselves and the people we are trying to help.

In the course of my work I have identified a number of negative approaches to the reconciliation process, unfortunately quite common. I am sure you will recognise the caricatures, but first take stock of your own tendencies.

In the following questionnaire, score yourself against each statement in this way:

5 if the statement generally applies to you
3 if the statement sometimes applies to you
0 if the statement rarely applies to you.

When I am faced with people engaged in conflict I would:

1   be quick to offer my services _____
2   act quickly to bring them together _____
3   try to separate them immediately _____
4   report the conflict at once _____
5   suggest that the parties sort the matter out as soon
    as possible _____
                                        Subtotal A _____

6   usually know who is in the wrong _____
7   support the weaker party _____
8   come down on the side of authority _____
9   turn a blind eye to it _____
10 try to judge who is in the right _____
                                        Subtotal B _____

11 look for the safest approach _____
12 be cautious about believing what was said _____
13 do some digging to find out the background _____
14 investigate what the parties said _____
15 seek to gain as much knowledge of the problems
    as possible _____
                                        Subtotal C _____

16 suggest a good book on resolving conflict _____
17 go away and think about it before acting _____
18 try to look at the problem from all angles _____
19 try to avoid getting involved, but would keep an
    eye on matters in case they got out of hand _____
20 remind the parties that this was no way for adults
    to behave _____
                                        Subtotal D _____

21 seek to get all the facts _____
22 look for the best way forward _____
23 check and double-check my information _____
24 move very cautiously at first _____
25 study the situation from a safe distance _____
                                        Subtotal E _____

26 look for the weakness in the parties' positions   _____
27 use my influence to bring the parties together   _____
28 look for a compromise   _____
29 find out what the price of peace was: everyone
    has their price   _____
30 seek to obtain agreement whatever the cost   _____

Subtotal F _____

31 try to impress on the parties the futility of conflict _____
32 go out of the way to help resolve the problem _____
33 use whatever leverage I could to end the conflict _____
34 appeal to their values as law-abiding citizens,
    Christians, etc   _____
35 emphasise the need for unity and harmony   _____

Subtotal G _____

36 move in and sort things out   _____
37 take prompt action if the conflict looked like
    getting out of hand   _____
38 only act if the conflict looked as if it would affect
    my interests   _____
39 support the person who was closest to my point
    of view   _____
40 confront both parties with their aggressive
    behaviour   _____

Subtotal H _____

INTERPRETATION

We'll now look in detail at the eight approaches to reconciliation which can cause problems. They are:

A The Ready Reconciler
B The Prejudiced Peacemaker
C The Cautious Conciliator
D The Reluctant Referee
E The Anxious Arbitrator
F The Cosy Compromiser
G The Missionary Mediator
H The Pragmatic Persuader.

How *badly* did you do? If you score 12 points or *more* on any single approach, then you need to apply the principles of *Peacing Together* more frequently. Read on and meet the misguided peacemakers!

THE READY RECONCILER

Always ready to jump in with both feet and solve problems, the Ready Reconciler is your real 'action' peacemaker. It doesn't take much to get him into full swing. His library contains such works as *Negotiation by Numbers, Multilateral Peacemaking for Undergraduates* and *Teach Yourself Middle-East Mediation*.

ALWAYS READY TO SWING INTO ACTION

THE PREJUDICED PEACEMAKER

Leaping to conclusions is the Prejudiced Peacemaker's real strength. Basing his approach on the smallest scrap of class, status, sexual, personal or financial bias, he will judge the rights and wrongs in the conflict before you can cry 'Discrimination!' His support can be bought readily, and he holds the *Guiness Book of Records* award for turning blind eyes to injustice, oppression and exploitation.

LEAPS TO CONCLUSIONS

THE CAUTIOUS CONCILIATOR

Having had his fingers burned many times, the Cautious Conciliator approaches conflict with great circumspection. He likes to have many facts at his fingertips and always carries his portable fire-fighting equipment to tackle unexpected conflicts that blaze up near him. Often his extreme caution and slow response allow small sparks of disagreement to flame up into great conflagrations. The Cautious Conciliator is, however, excellent at raking through the burned-out ruins of a relationship and giving detailed explanations as to the source of the conflict.

POST MORTEMS A SPECIALITY

'WHAT YOU SHOULD HAVE DONE WAS...'

THE RELUCTANT REFEREE

This gentleman is a skilled peacemaker. At least—he has all the books and knows all the rules and procedures for managing conflict. His fascination with the theory, however, prevents him from playing any active role in the reconciliation process. He is happy to sit on the sidelines and observe the action from a distance. He is a good reference point, and after the conflict has been solved will give any number of pieces of advice as to what ought to have been done.

THE ANXIOUS ARBITRATOR

He is closely related to the Reluctant Referee, though this chap does get involved...eventually. He only acts once he has studied the origins of the conflict and the background of the parties in fine detail. He is particularly in his element when the source of the conflict can be traced to written documents, which he then delights in perusing. The Anxious Arbitrator radiates a love for small print.

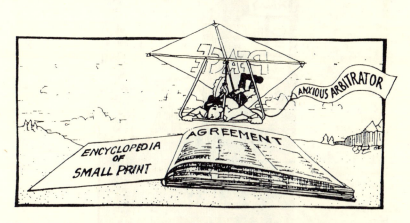

HOLDS WORLD RECORD FOR HOVERING IMMOBILE OVER SMALL PRINT

THE COSY COMPROMISER

'Live and let live' is the watch-cry of the Cosy Compromiser. She offers a give-and-take solution to all differences of opinion. She encourages parties to give ground to gain a compromise, but both end up losing. The Cosy Compromiser plays to the weaknesses of the parties, and to their fear of exposure.

PEACE... AT ANY PRICE

BOLDLY GOING WHERE NO
MEDIATOR HAS GONE BEFORE

THE MISSIONARY MEDIATOR

The zealous peacemaking of the Missionary Mediator is world famous: reaching out to conflicts where no conflicts have ever been before is his forte. His strong belief in peace and harmony ensure that no conflict will go unchallenged, and that all parties will be quickly brought to understand the error of their ways. Inexperienced Missionary Mediators often end up being eaten in the conflict jungle.

THE PRAGMATIC PERSUADER

THE PRAGMATIC PERSUADER

That conflicts are bad and need to be ended quickly is the basic tenet of the Pragmatic Persuader. It doesn't matter what means are used, just as long as the end is peaceful. Simple, direct approaches are preferred!

Summary

We need to be honest and well-informed about the barriers to reconciliation. Bad timing, long distances, lack of opportunity, anxiety about public image and false expectations — all can stand between ourselves and peace. But not all the barriers are quite so obvious: many more lie within: fear of the unknown, mistrust of everyone involved, and personality traits which — although we can laugh at them in the cartoons and caricatures drawn here — may sometimes be seriously destructive to peace.

CHAPTER EIGHT

THE RISKS OF RECONCILIATION

Some conflicts are well managed and lead to situations in which everyone is better off. Some are badly managed and lead to situations in which either everyone is worse off or someone is a little better off and someone is a little worse off.[1]

I N THE PREVIOUS CHAPTER though we considered barriers to reconciliation, we saw that these barriers may also be used to *prevent* conflict escalation. In fact, time, distance, lack of opportunity and public image, are all powerful tools to keep the parties under control, and in the hands of a skilled reconciler can ensure that uncontrolled explosions do not take place. But a battlefield is a dangerous place, and the reconciler must step warily.

Analysis of the Situation

Since conflict is always hurtful (and in that sense there are no winners), and since there is no guarantee that reconciliation will work, there is a high risk that the wounds could be deepened as a result of attempts to bring peace. So the peacemaker must first analyse the positions and strategies of the parties in conflict.

In deciding which strategies to use, the mediator should bear in mind that parties in conflict can be influenced by one or more of eight major considerations.

1 Their aims
2 Their values
3 Their strengths
4 Their weaknesses
5 Their opportunities
6 Their risks
7 The timing
8 The climate.

We shall look at each in turn.

Since each conflict is unique, there may well be other avenues open to the peacemaker which can be explored so that the parties move closer together. Clearly, not all possibilities have the same weight in all situations.

AIMS

What are the conflicting parties attempting to achieve? What are their desired outcomes from the conflict? Do you as peacemaker know what 'success' would mean — for each party?

These important questions must be thought through. Would it be sufficient for the enemy to 'go away'? Would a full surrender with apologies all round be their minimum aim? Is total destruction of the opposition the goal? We must be clear about everyone's aims, since these will influence our strategy of reconciliation. The aims are linked with the phase that the conflict has reached. In phase one I am prepared to live and let live, but in phase three, I want the other party to lose; my aim is his destruction.

VALUES

The parties' values will influence their own choice of strategy in the conflict. A 'peace at any price' philosophy will restrict the opposition's approach to conflict and deny them most of the tactics commonly used in hostilities (described in Chapter Twelve). On the other hand, a strong sense of rightness in their cause, coupled with a view that wrong should be punished, may cause them to extend the conflict beyond a partial resolution into a reign of terror in which all who opposed them, and even those neutral who did not support them, are systematically finished off for their sins! The Stalin era was a period of great pain in 'peace' for the nations of the USSR.

STRENGTHS AND WEAKNESSES

What are the strengths of the parties in conflict? Think of one conflict of which you are currently aware and make a list of the strengths of each party. In the same way, consider the weaknesses in the positions of each party. Strengths and weaknesses relate primarily to the *present* situation— to where the parties are now, as a result of their experiences to date. But of course no analysis is complete without an examination of possible future developments.

OPPORTUNITIES

What opportunities exist? What could each party do as a result of its present position and strengths? What initiatives are possible in the light of the strengths and weaknesses of the opposition?

Taking account of the opposition's aims, where might they try to move to next? These questions will lead the peacemaker to the consideration of a number of options, each of which must be further examined for likelihood of success, taking into account, of course, the possible risks. Thinking through the positions of the parties enables the peacemaker to take and keep the initiative.

RISKS

The weaknesses and the strengths of the parties are two major sources of risk. What can be done to minimise the exposure of each party, particularly the weaker side? Are there any ways in which we could alter the positions and strengths of the opposing parties to make them more equal?

Samson had a weakness which was exploited by his enemies.[2] We all are vulnerable on some front. Both parties may become so weakened that they end up as targets for a third and previously unnoticed enemy. The skill of the peacemaker is, in part, to be able to identify the risks of continued conflict. He must then use these risks to constrain the parties from further conflict.

TIMING

Timing affects everything. When is the best time for the peacemaker to participate in the reconciliation process? We should avoid being drawn into confrontation before we are ready. Jesus knew when his time had come—until then he would not be drawn into his final conflict,[3] though he took every opportunity to state the claims of God and the kingdom, to both friend and foe alike.

THE CLIMATE

In families, relationships, churches, organisations and nations, there are times when conflict will grow out of control. Northern Ireland is one historical example of a situation in which the climate is still ripe for conflict but not yet for reconciliation. When everyone is at war with everyone else, who is left to pick up the pieces? In such a situation the parties devour one another and anything else in the way. In such environments there is only one strategy for the peacemaker: to withdraw until the time is right. So before we rush out and try to stop a conflict, we need to ask ourselves these ten questions. If we cannot answer 'yes' to them all, we should think again before we act.

TEN QUESTIONS BEFORE WE BEGIN RECONCILIATION

1 Have I counted the costs to myself?
2 Is the time right?
3 Am I acceptable to both sides?
4 Is my aim clear?
5 Do I have the initiative?
6 Will my next move be supported by both parties?
7 Is my strategy simple?
8 Is my position consolidated?
9 Can I withstand a surprise attack?
10 Am I well supported?

The progress of both conflict and reconciliation is influenced by the internal and external constraints experienced on both sides. The peacemaker may wish to speed up or slow down the process. This may be necessary when the two parties experience different reactions—say—to the confessions: one may be greatly relieved to get the issue off her conscience, whereas the other may be greatly angered by the new disclosure. The peacemaker may then want to separate the parties for a while.

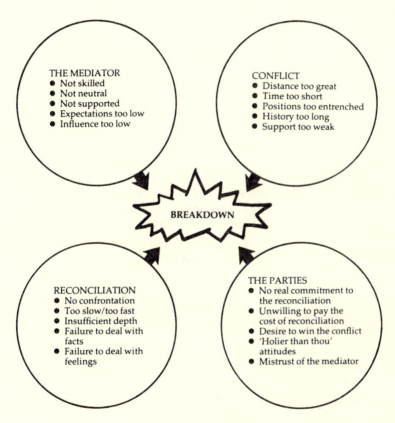

THE MEDIATOR
- Not skilled
- Not neutral
- Not supported
- Expectations too low
- Influence too low

CONFLICT
- Distance too great
- Time too short
- Positions too entrenched
- History too long
- Support too weak

BREAKDOWN

RECONCILIATION
- No confrontation
- Too slow/too fast
- Insufficient depth
- Failure to deal with facts
- Failure to deal with feelings

THE PARTIES
- No real commitment to the reconciliation
- Unwilling to pay the cost of reconciliation
- Desire to win the conflict
- 'Holier than thou' attitudes
- Mistrust of the mediator

The Failure of Peace

Failure

That the natural outcome of conflict is not reconciliation but more conflict was one of the earlier conclusions of this book. So what causes failure? Its origins lie in the parties themselves, the kind of conflict, and the mediator. The diagram on page 135 shows the major factors which contribute to the breakdown of reconciliation attempts.

Summary

Peacemakers must not underestimate the barriers they face in bringing people to real peace. Thus a thorough and realistic assessment of the state of conflict is essential. The peacemaker should produce a written description of the position of the two parties. In complex conflicts it is helpful for the peacemaker to try to 'role play' the two positions before he attempts to become involved. This can be done by putting two chairs back to back. The peacemaker should sit in one chair and describe (out loud helps) the position of the first party as he sees it. Then, transferring to the other chair, the peacemaker attempts to describe the position of the other party. If the peacemaker cannot make a reasonable job of describing *both* parties' positions, he needs to do more work to understand how the parties view themselves. Only when the peacemaker understands both positions will he be able to anticipate the barriers.

We must not forget, either, that one barrier to achieving real peace is the tendency of the peacemaker to become weary of the task. Reconciliation demands much of the peacemaker. A tired peacemaker makes mistakes, fails to notice critical signals from the parties and is unable to maintain the initiative.

Let's now examine in more detail the costs of reconciliation and look at some ways in which the cost can be shared so that the process is made easier.

CHAPTER NINE

THE PRICE OF RECONCILIATION

To hope is a duty not a luxury
To hope is not a dream, but to turn dream
into reality.
Happy are those who dream dreams and
are ready to pay the price to make
them come true.[1]

T HROUGHOUT THE AGES the human race has sought
ways of creating peace. When faced with the sabre-
toothed tiger, man had two options—fight or flight.
To fight put life at risk, and flight, if fast enough,
only put dignity at risk! Either way a cost had to be paid.

When faced with less tangible enemies—sickness,
disease, famine, drought—the fight/flight response did
not work for our ancestors, nor does it for us. Invisible
spirits of evil could not be confronted, nor could one run
from them. A different price had to be paid—either to
those who had the power to take away the evil spirits, or
directly to the angry spiritual dignitaries whose wrath had
caused the discomfort. A libation, an offering, a sacrifice
appeased them and brought hope of peace.

Faced today with conflict on all fronts, we still retain that
hope of peace—if not in our time, at least in the times of
our children's children. For the present, we hope for a
containment of conflict on the global scale; but the cost is
enormous. So too at the personal level the cost of containing
conflict is high, but the cost of reconciliation may be higher!

No Credit

Martin Luther King's dream cost him his life. Ghandi, Sadat, Scott of the Antarctic, Joan of Arc, tens of thousands of the Crusaders, St Peter, St Paul—men and women down through the centuries give us examples of people whose dreams were compelling enough to call for the ultimate sacrifice. And at the heart of the Christian faith lies the event which represents the great cost of reconciliation; 'We were reconciled to him [to God] through the death of his Son.[2]

We live at a time when immediate gratification is the norm. 'Live now, pay later' is the philosophy. With borrowing and indebtedness never higher at both the personal and national levels, the world lives on credit. In the realm of peace, however, there is no credit. Peace requires a down payment, then regular instalments throughout the reconciliation. Even then there is no guarantee that the goods will be forthcoming; we may pay in full; we may pay over and over again and still be denied the elusive prize of real peace. This is particularly so for peacemakers and mediators whose tasks, mission and dream it is to help bring peace in conflict.

What does it take to be a peacemaker? How much does it cost to bring peace? What skills are needed? These are the questions I will try to answer in this chapter. They are crucial, for as we saw, 'confession', 'repentance' and 'forgiveness' are words that have been rejected in our generation. We have discovered too that peace is not possible if we want it instantly and freely. We cannot afford to say, 'If I cannot have it now and without charge, then I don't want it at all.' Such sentiments prevent peace and dishearten the would-be peacemaker.

Faced with parties who want cheap peace, the peacemaker may have to pay the first set of instalments himself. These early payments have to do with taking risks; taking initiative and confronting the parties, for, as Moses found out over 4,000 years ago, being a peacemaker can put us at the wrong end of the firing line![3] Later payments involve careful planning and realistic expectations of the sacrifices involved, but let us look first at the early instalments.

Risk

Conflicts are dangerous. The participants get hurt; even the innocent bystanders get hurt. Children get dragged into husband-and-wife conflicts. Civilians get blown up in supermarkets, airports and planes as terrorists extend their violence indiscriminately. And peacemakers get caught in the crossfire from entrenched positions. These risks are inherent in the role—a role that develops either formally or informally.

THE FORMAL ROLE

The formal role of the peacemaker is usually associated with position, status or experience. In the formal role the peacemaker is invited to work with the parties. In this formal role, the peacemaker may have little to lose. His reputation is already established: if he fails, the failure can be blamed on the parties; if he is successful, it is because he is a good peacemaker! He may face the professional disappointment which accompanies an abortive initiative, but it can all be put down to experience. So, for the peacemaker, a formal role offers some security.

THE INFORMAL ROLE

The informal role represents a much higher level of risk. In this situation the peacemaker is more likely to become involved because of personal interests. Perhaps the peacemaker knows the parties. He may be concerned at an emotional level for their peace and may already have established relationships with one or both sides. Here, then, the risks are much higher, for even a successful reconciliation may be at the expense of the peacemaker's own relationships with one or both parties. Certainly, failure of the reconciliation will increase the circle of mutual blame and recrimination and embrace the would-be peacemaker. The parties may even project on to the peacemaker the blame for the irreconcilable breakdown!

Whether his role is formal or informal, the peacemaker runs the risk of being used by either party for its own ends.

Parties may see the peacemaker as likely to achieve what they have been unable to achieve alone—victory. Or they may use the peacemaker to 'disarm' the opposition, to lull them into a false sense of security prior to a surprise attack. Or they may disagree on the role of the peacemaker and simply do away with him. It appeared to most people that Terry Waite, the Archbishop of Canterbury's special envoy, was operating in an informal role on behalf of the Western hostages in Lebanon. Nevertheless, he was viewed very differently by both sides. The magnitude of that difference did not surface until after his abduction.

A peacemaking role is costly. It may cost our family or our friends. It will put them all at risk emotionally as they worry over our well-being when we step into a 'war' zone.

Initiative

The year 1987 saw the death in Spandau prison, Berlin, of the last of the Third Reich hierarchy—Rudolf Hess. From my childhood home in Glasgow I could look across the environs of the city to the hills on which, on 10th May 1941 Hess crash-landed his Messerscmitt 110 plane. He claimed to be on a peace initiative. It was reported that Hess had come to negotiate peace with the British government. Whatever the real purpose of his mission, the Russians believe that Hess came to negotiate peace in Western Europe so that Germany could concentrate its full power on the Russian front. He was imprisoned in Britain during the remainder of the war and then spent the rest of his life in solitary confinement until he took his own life at the age of ninety-two. The Hess story graphically illustrates the risks to the initiators: misunderstanding, mistrust and isolation. Whatever Hess' real mission, it failed. No one believed or supported him.[4]

When I was seven my father took me on a day's outing by bus and by foot across the moors to the spot where the plane had crashed. But that wasn't where the Hess mission had failed, for it had failed at the conceptual stage. The timing was wrong, and Hess had no role—formal or informal. His desire for peace, if such it was, led him to a high-risk initiative which foundered. Would he have done it again knowing that the odds were so high against him? Would you? The true peacemaker would reply, 'It might just work. The benefits to others outweigh any price that I might have to pay. Let's go! All peace initiatives are fraught with danger.'

Confrontation

Peacemaking is obviously no soft option. The peacemaker is a person of inner strength. Confrontation requires a rare inner resolve, as we shall see in Chapter Ten. True, there are many examples of confrontation as people aggressively seek to achieve their own aims, but useful and genuine confrontation in the context of peacemaking is not selfish. Instead it is bent towards considering the other party. Confrontation requires the peacemaker to take the risk of facing the parties' destructive behaviour.

The prophets of the Old Testament were confronters: sometimes their confrontation led to peace, but more often the reaction to their challenge was hostile, and the prophets paid for their initiatives with liberty and, in some cases, life. Nathan confronted a warrior king with his crimes of adultery and murder.[5] His initiative was successful because his role and power were recognised; the time was also right. The response to Jeremiah's confrontation was less reasonable but more predictable. He was thrown into prison to silence him.[6] But peace was too important for him and even from the dungeon he sought to confront the nation's leaders.

Confrontation of the hostile parties by the mediator can be the trigger that signals a ceasefire, but with the risks of retaliation being high, the peacemaker has no guarantee of safe passage. Nor can the peacemaker afford to cloak his intentions. He must be open about his desire for peace.

Planning for Reconciliation

Reconciliation does not, as we have seen, just happen. The true peacemaker *works* to achieve openness. He develops a clear, flexible strategy for dealing with the natural resistances on both sides. He is sensitive both to the parties themselves and to the multiple relationships involved. He is also conscious of the need for listening, for confidentiality, for expressing his own feelings; and he considers the proper environment for the convergence of the two parties. In all he does, he tries to model to the two sides the kind of open behaviour he wants to elicit from them.

OPENNESS

Conflicts are breeding-grounds for deception, intrigue and disinformation (a deliberate spreading of false information). The peacemaker needs to model new behaviour, to set new standards of openness, directness and trust. Stereotypes, the assumptions, the prejudices need to be broken down; openness is the best course. Such openness is in keeping with risk-taking, initiative and confrontation. It is vital for the parties to see an example of openness, for they too will have to go through a process of revelation before reconciliation is achieved. A peacemaker who tries to manipulate the parties covertly will only reinforce the patterns of avoidance already used by the conflicting parties. Even when the mediator sets the pattern of behaviour, his messages will rarely be received the first time. He will have to show and show again the models of behaviour needed for the restoration of peace.

RESISTANCE

It is rare for reconciliation to proceed without setbacks. The peacemaker often has to learn as he goes along. His experience will help him identify the likely barriers and problems, but inevitably each conflict is unique and each reconciliation presents its own special difficulties. At each step in the reconciliation process, the parties will try to find ways of avoiding the costs of rebuilding their relationships. Consciously or unconsciously, though they want reconciliation, they do not want it at any price, but preferably at no cost at all.

Sometimes it will be a case of one step forward and two back. This is often so when the period of reconciliation is lengthy. The memory of what the conflict cost begins to fade, and there is a temptation to slip back into the fighting mode. Setbacks are common, so the peacemaker will need persistence, tenacity and endurance. These qualities emerge as a result of total commitment to reconciliation. Peace-making is not for the faint-hearted! Yet it is not a blind obstinacy that is required. It is a perceptive and creative determination to help the parties re-establish their unity. In this and other ways, the peacemaker needs to be a planner and an organiser.

FLEXIBILITY

Though it is true that reconciliations are not unknown at funerals or during other family crises, in these circum-stances the differences are only pushed aside long enough for the parties to recognise their common ground, but we cannot wait for a handy funeral to stage our reconciliations! We need to have a flexible, viable plan.

We saw in Chapter Six that for reconciliation to be re-alised, there are three major phases to be gone through: disengagement, convergence and integration. The peace-maker must plan his strategy and timing such that all these phases happen in sequence. The timing needs to be flexible since the rate of progress through each phase and step is unpredictable. The Iran/Iraq war went on for years without ceasefire—phase one, step one. Berlin has been a divided city since 1945—phase one, step two! The Anglican Church split from the Roman Catholic Church some 400 years ago, but at least they have stopped burning one another's priests at the stake! In fact, Anglicans and Roman Catholics have recently come so close together that they could publish a joint document called Anglican-Roman Catholic Inter-national Commission—*The Final Report*—which spells out common points of conviction and vision for the future of the Christian church in the world. Published in 1982, this report concluded:

Christian hope manifests itself in prayer and action—in prudence but also in courage. We pledge ourselves and exhort the faithful of the Roman Catholic Church and of the Anglican Communion to live and work courageously in this hope of reconciliation and unity in our common Lord.[7]

Convergence, step three! The steps may be a long time in coming, but there is a time for every step in reconciliation, and it is the task of the peacemaker to synchronise the steps with the readiness of the parties.

When should the parties meet? Where and for how long? Who else should be present, and what should be their roles? Who should speak first, and what should be the agenda? When that first meeting is over, what will be the next step, and how long before it is taken? These are the primary concerns of the peacemaker as he organises the process for the restoration of peace.

SENSITIVITY

Patience is also required. Although progress may be slow, each meeting gives the peacemaker an opportunity to strengthen his understanding of the parties and to build his relationship and role with them.

His task is to cause a meeting of minds and hearts. During the conflict, in order to reduce their hurt, the combatants have built around themselves protective shells. Like scallops or snails, they protect themselves from injury. People locked in combat find contact with another person is a source of pain, so they try to avoid contact at almost any cost.

There is a dilemma here, for in order to bring the parties to reconciliation the peacemaker needs to establish direct contact between the parties as soon as possible. Yet their defences cannot be torn down; they must dismantle their protective barriers at their own speed. The need for defence has been real. They have been subject to genuine attacks— and may yet be again if reconciliation breaks down; therefore, the relationship-building must be slow, steady and sure. Sharing is the principal key to improving the relationship between the parties. Without a firmly laid foundation in phase two, it is unlikely that the final phase of integration will be successful. How may the relationship be improved during phase two? The facts, the feelings and the vision which are shared become the building-blocks of the new foundation, but the cement which binds these together is the skill of listening. This has been badly damaged in the course of the conflict.

SENSORY DEPRIVATION

Foundries and weaving sheds were the causes of more industrial deafness than any other workplaces. The continuous pounding of the forge hammers and the rattle of the shuttle boxes produced noise levels in excess of 100 decibels. The noise hurt! After prolonged exposure, workers suffered permanent damage to their hearing. Protection is now mandatory; all workers in these environments are required to wear 'muffs' or ear plugs that reduce the wearers' exposure to damaging noise levels. Sadly, a peculiar phenomenon is experienced by some who wear noise protection devices over long periods; they begin to hear phantom noises—usually voices or music. Sufferers can be seen tapping out rhythms in time to the music in their heads. The phenomenon is a mild version of what is experienced in the early stages of total sensory deprivation.

Conflict has a similar effect on its participants. Prolonged exposure reduces the capacity to listen and hear. Instead of receiving painful messages, they begin to switch off and ignore the communications which hurt them. As with the prolonged use of ear protection, the parties in conflict will begin to 'hear their own messages'—imagining innuendoes, slights and insults in every exchange with the opponent. With such impaired listening on both sides, the peacemaker will have to assist the process of reintroducing them to open communication. With damaged listening skills, they will be unable to participate in the sharing required in phase two of the reconciliation process. The burden of improving communications will fall initially on the peacemaker, as he ensures that the sharing of facts and feelings is complete.

In *Team Spirit* I deal extensively with the improvement of listening skills. One section which people have found particularly useful deals with the ten commandments for effective listening, which are reproduced below.[8]

The Commandments for Listening

1 Do be prepared to work hard at listening.
2 Do keep an open mind.
3 Do beware of hearing only what you want or expect to hear, and don't make assumptions about what people are going to say.
4 Do listen to *how* things are said, but don't spend your time mentally criticising the way a contribution is being presented.
5 Do withhold judgement or evaluation until the entire point has been presented.
6 Do ask for clarification if you have not understood.
7 Don't be afraid to admit you 'switched off' for a minute or misheard.
8 Don't think about *your* next contribution while another person is talking.
9 Don't interrupt, and don't finish people's sentences for them—you could be wrong.
10 Don't react emotionally to personal 'red-flag' words.

I find that the relearning of basic listening skills is one of the most difficult and frustrating aspects of reconciliation. The peacemaker faces more failures due to the inability of the parties to communicate than due to any other problem. But listening is only one side of the communication barrier. As the inability to hear exists on one side, so on the other is the inability to remain silent.

CONFIDENTIALITY

We once had a neighbour who was known in the village as *The News of the World*. He was a walking broadcasting service! Whatever he knew he passed on, and what he didn't know he made up in the most creative way he could and then passed on!

During interpersonal conflict, information and misinformation are often used as weapons to strengthen the rightness of positions and undermine the credibility of the opposition; hence new behaviours must be adopted. Trust must be built up, and the confidentiality of the process must be assured before embarking on the sharing activities of phase two.

Sanctions for breaking confidentiality may have to be laid down by the peacemaker and guarantees obtained of the parties' secrecy during the process. Even then there are risks to the participants: first, that one party will break the confidentiality and use information shared during reconciliation to heighten the conflict; second, that there will be no reconciliation, the process breaking down with the opponents knowing a lot more sensitive and personal data about each other. In the Rekyiavik summit of 1986 between Ronald Reagan and Mikhail Gorbachev, a media silence was maintained throughout the extended meetings, but immediately the talks had ended in deadlock, the Soviet premier laid the blame for failure at the door of the American president, claiming that Reagan had no power to negotiate. This may have been true, but it was also a breach of trust and embarrassed the US president.

During reconciliation, confidentiality must be maintained; all information shared, both facts and feelings, must remain confidential to the parties involved. A large number of reconciliation attempts break down because parties share confidential information with people outside the process. Perhaps they see a secret as something to share with 'just' one person at a time, or perhaps they find the reconciliation process so lonely that they feel the urge to talk with anyone is irresistible. So the peacemaker needs to ensure that the parties understand the meaning of the word 'confidential', and he will also need to be the confidant who hears and shares the loneliness of the parties locked into the silence of agreed confidentiality.

The peacemaker himself faces another problem in the area of confidentiality. I have been involved in a number of reconciliation processes in which some disclosures and confessions were made that took me by surprise. Some were deeply disturbing. At the time of the confessions, the peacemaker has of course to concentrate on helping the parties to hear, understand and forgive; but the peacemaker cannot deny his own feelings. What do we do with our own shock reactions? How do we cope with our own feelings and emotions?

The title *Peacing Together* declares that reconciliation, peacemaking and mediation should all be based on teamwork. We should not be tempted to go it alone. We shall look at teamwork more closely in later chapters, but it is enough to indicate here that the team does allow the peacemaker to brief his support group, who act as co-reconcilers, although they may never actually sit down with the parties in conflict. The team is there to support the frontline peacemaker and to help him (in strict confidence, of course) to deal with his own feelings arising from the disturbing confidential data. The peacemaker can help the individuals come to terms with the revelation only if he can come to terms with the data himself.

EMOTION

Coming to terms with confessions it not easy. There has grown up over the years an image of the peacemaker as a cool, objective, detached, untouched-by-it-all stoic. It is true that the peacemaker is not there to be a judge or arbitrate between the parties; nevertheless, the peacemaker also has feelings. As we have seen, the peacemaker too faces anger, frustration, disappointment, elation, warmth and affection in relation to the reconciling parties.

One school of teaching suggests that the peacemaker should show no emotion during his or her counselling of the parties. In fact I have found this 'objectivity' to be more of a hindrance. In the presence of a detached peacemaker parties will take much longer to express their own feelings—if they ever do at all. Again, it is my experience that the peacemaker will have more success if he can model the behaviour he expects from the people in conflict. The peacemaker needs both parties to share facts and feelings, so he must share, too—facts about the conflict, and feelings about the process. The peacemaker needs the parties to focus on the future and to build a common vision of a thoroughly changed relationship, so he must set the example—giving positive feedback and encouragement to the parties when they move forward, and expressing his own disappointment or frustration when the parties display a lack of trust or commitment.

We cannot come close to people who are hurting and not be touched by their pain. The Good Samaritan, coming alongside the injured man, had to walk all the way to Jericho and spend his own resources so that the man might be healed.[9] As one writer put it:

Wanted: Peacemakers

Caring people who dare to be present with people when they are hurting and dare to stand with people where they are hurting. Peacemaking begins by truly being there for others.[10]

To weep with those who weep and to rejoice with those who rejoice is one of the great compensations for the peace-maker. Without emotion there can be no peace. Peace-making is a sensitive and emotional business.

Summary

Reconciliation is not cheap. It costs a lot. All those involved, particularly the peacemaker, will need to pay part of the price of peace to minimise the cost. The peacemaker needs to develop certain skills and should never work alone. With a team supporting his efforts, the strains, stresses and emotions can be shared. Also, the joys of the reconciliation can be communicated to others—reinforcing the worth-whileness of the long, lonely journey that is the pilgrimage to reconciliation.

CHAPTER TEN

KEEPING THE PEACE

To the people of all nations in the hope that within a century there will no longer be a Veterans Day Parade but that there will be lots of living people left to march to a different drum because all the world loves a parade.[1]

PEACE IS NECESSARY for reconciliation, and since reconciliation takes time, the peacemaker must learn to keep the peace long enough for reconciliation to take place. The early hours of the ceasefire are the most precarious. An accidental shot, an unexplained or misinterpreted action, rumour and mistrust—all can trigger conflict again.

'Blessed are the peacemakers, for they will be called sons of God.' So states St Matthew in his account of the Sermon on the Mount.[2] Peacemaking is a skilled activity and clearly—according to Jesus' words—a highly valued activity. In this chapter we shall look at ways in which the peacemaker can operate effectively. The aim of the peacemaker is not simply to contain, control and limit the damage of the conflict, but to achieve a lasting reconciliation of the parties.

The Conflict Cycle

In his book *Interpersonal Peacemaking*, Richard Walton[3] observes that conflict between individuals is usually cyclical rather than linear. At times the conflict lies dormant only to flare up in overt aggression then die down again. This cyclical movement presents the peacemaker with a variety of opportunities and targets for his initiatives. But, before we examine the possible approaches, let us look at the cycles that make up the spiral. There are four elements to each cycle of the spiral: the issues, the triggers, the behaviours and the consequences.

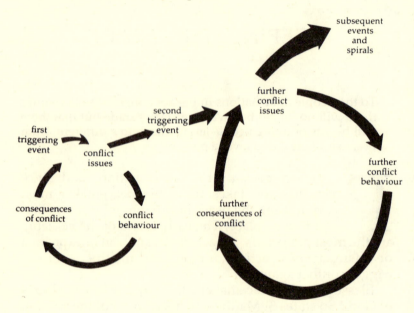

The Spiral of Conflict

CONFLICT ISSUES

As we have seen, the conflict issues may be substantive or subjective. Substantive issues (you will recall) involve disagreement over facts, events, objects, roles, practices etc, such as 'I do not want you to introduce new ideas in the church, and I will oppose you every time you make a move to change things.' Subjective issues involve feelings between parties—fear, distrust, resentment, rejection etc. For example, 'I think that you despise me, and each time I meet you I feel angry and resentful towards you.' Substantive issues are objective; subjective issues are usually emotional, although there is generally a large overlap.

A priority for the peacemaker is to discover the exact nature of the issue. In long-standing conflicts the opponents will often have lost sight of the substantive origins of the conflict, if there ever were any, and the peacemaker may have a lot of work to do to uncover the roots of the antagonism.

TRIGGER EVENTS

Subjective or objective, many conflicts are suppressed, and for most of the time a casual observer sees nothing wrong in the relationship. The latent conflict may only flare up as the result of a triggering event. The event can be a word, a look, a mannerism or something much more obvious in the way of an act of aggression, invasion or assault. You may arrest one of my spies, deport one of my diplomats, carry out a cross-border raid, raise the price of goods, introduce a new hymn book, or criticise my mother-in-law. Anything may trigger my response. Obviously in the area of emotional conflicts the stimuli may be very difficult to identify. Nevertheless, it is important to try to establish the nature of the triggers. A knowledge of the triggers will enable the peacemaker to:

1 Avoid or precipitate confrontation during the process of reconciliation—as appropriate.
2 Understand better the issues of the conflict.
3 Manage the reconciliation process more effectively.
4 Help the parties cope better with their emotions and behaviour.

CONFLICT BEHAVIOUR

The trigger causes one or both parties to respond. Their behaviour will, in turn, be dictated by the level of the conflict. Are the exchanges non-verbal, verbal or physical? What is the scope of the conflict? Does it involve one difference or many? Are the parties in danger of doing themselves and others permanent damage?

Once again, the precise type of conflict behaviour needs to be identified and understood by the peacemaker. Is it arguing, criticising, blaming, challenging, creating wider division, taking sides or undermining?

The peacemaker will then confront the parties with their behaviour: 'This is what you are doing.' Feedback must be 'here-and-now' rather than 'then-and-there'. In Chapter Twelve I will enlarge on the most common conflict behaviours and show how the peacemaker might respond.

CONSEQUENCES

The behaviours inevitably have far-reaching effects. As we have said, the cost not only to the parties themselves but to innocent bystanders can be very distressing. Olive Schreiner, writing in 1911, reminded the people of that generation that the effects of conflict reach far beyond the war zone. 'There is no battlefield on earth, nor ever has been, howsoever covered with slain, which has not cost the women of the race more in actual bloodshed and anguish to supply, than it has cost the men who lie there.[4]

Thus, by drawing attention to the wider consequences of the conflict, the peacemaker can often gain a temporary truce. The 'peace' thus obtained can then be used to move the parties down the reconciliation road.

The Next Cycle

Without a cessation of hostilities, the consequences of the first cycle will simply be added to the issues of the conflict. Both sides become more sensitive and react to a wider spectrum of triggers. Thus the balance between peace and conflict becomes increasingly precarious. It will take less provocation to trigger the second cycle.

In further turns of the spiral the behaviour will worsen according to the pattern that we saw in Chapter One. In turn the consequences will be even more far-reaching, resulting in a further increase of issues.

PROLIFERATION OF ISSUES

One difficulty the peacemaker faces in bringing about a reconciliation is the fact that conflict spirals are dynamic— they move very rapidly—worsening and lessening moment by moment. Timing of the intervention by the peacemaker is therefore critical. A second difficulty, which is linked to the dynamic nature of conflict, is the tendency of the parties to proliferate the issues—enlarge them, multiply them and even invent them. Proliferation comes in a number of forms and the peacemaker must be able to recognise them.

Legitimising the issues. In this mode one or both parties attempts to justify their position by reference to a larger or higher principle. 'It says in the Bible/constitution/argreement etc. . . ' or 'There is a precedent for my position', etc.

Substitution brings into the conflict an issue which one party feels stronger about but which has no real connection with the root issue. 'That's typical of your family! Your mother was the same!'

Screening. This is an attempt to cover vulnerability and to move the issue to some other less embarrassing topic. 'The real issue is not whether I'm angry, but whether there are enough spaces in the car park!'

Duplication. Here the parties use another but similar issue as the pretext for the conflict. 'We're *not* going to your mother's again. It's far too long to drive.'

Packaging. In this form the parties use the conflict to bring in a whole series of issues and settle old scores. 'And while we're at it, back in 1926 I remember you. . . .'

Achilles' heel, in which one party will switch the issue to focus on the other party's weakness. 'There is no point in trying to discuss this with you—you're drunk!'

These tactics must be recognised and dealt with directly if progress is to be made. The peacemaker must be able to confront the parties with their proliferation tactics and bring them back to the root issue.

Managing the Conflict

If the time is not right for reconciliation because one or both parties are still on a win/lose course, then the peacemaker may have to be content with and concentrate on containment measures. The following list offers some useful approaches:

1   Reduce the frequency of heated encounters by separating the parties or being there when the parties meet. This places constraints on them.

2   Intervene at the first sign of a trigger.

3   Create as many barriers to conflict as possible.

4   Give the parties separate opportunities to express their feelings. This prevents the conflict being suppressed and reduces the chance of an uncontrollable outburst, or excessive stress.

5   Agree a cooling-off period as a prelude to the reconciliation discussions.

6   Legislate the type of behaviour which is acceptable/not acceptable to the wider group, eg no chemical or nuclear weapons to be used; no confrontations in or after church; no strikes, lockouts or threats etc.

7   Ask the parties to write down their own descriptions of the situation: their hopes, fears and position.

8   Increase the parties' tolerance of conflict by giving emotional support to *both* sides.

9   Creatively explore possibilities for new solutions.

10   In situations where it is appropriate, encourage the parties to pray first separately with the peacemaker and then together with him. The prayer of St Francis, page 12, is often acceptable, whatever the religious background.

It should be remembered that the above are containment strategies and do not necessarily lead to reconciliation. Eventually the parties must be brought face to face and the conflict confronted squarely.

Preparing for Confrontation

Confrontation is a highly successful approach to the resolution of conflict. By 'confrontation' I mean the process by which both parties directly face the issues of the conflict in an attempt to clarify the issues and the feelings of the situation. However, because it has aggressive aspects to it, confrontation needs to take place in a controlled environment. The confrontation may be on a one-to-one basis, but is more likely to be successful with the help or even at the instigation of a peacemaker. A number of features can contribute to a positive confrontation.

MUTUAL DESIRE FOR PEACE

Both parties must be willing to say, 'We cannot go on like this.' If one party has more to gain by continuing the conflict, then the aggression will dominate. The peacemaker can help by emphasising the losses of the conflict and stressing the benefits of co-operation.

EQUALITY OF POWER

If there is an imbalance of power, then the chance that trust will develop is reduced, and openness is inhibited. The peacemaker should attempt to reduce the imbalance by emphasising the interdependence of the parties. He could also foster the security of the weaker party by giving extra support or through ground rule advantages. For example, each party could be given no more time than the other to express his point. Or perhaps a meeting could take place in a location which favours the weaker party.

MUTUALLY AGREEABLE TIMING

Both parties must be ready to confront and to be confronted. If one party is not prepared, then the conflict may begin again; the avoidance of one party may be seen as a vindication of the position held by the other confronting party. Subsequent attempts to confront the problem jointly will be more difficult.

Two-Phase Procedure

A confrontation meeting should have two main phases. In the first, the parties are encouraged to gain a clearer understanding of the differences which separate them—this is called the *differentiation phase*. The behaviour in this first phase may be more aggressive than assertive. In the second phase the parties are encouraged to look for common ground and common goals—this is called the *integration phase*. A series of differentiation/integration exchanges may be necessary before the parties can be reconciled, but it is essential that the phases be synchronised. If one party is trying to look for common ground while the other is still trying to emphasise the differences, then both will experience frustration and failure. The peacemaker must ensure that the two parties engage in the same activities at the same time.

A Supportive Environment

Confrontation requires openness between the parties. The atmosphere will be heavily influenced by the preparation and attitude of the peacemaker. Openness requires skill and sensitivity, both of which the conflicting parties lack. The peacemaker may therefore need to work with the parties individually before bringing them together. This preparation will improve their ability to express feelings, give and receive comments and handle sensitive disclosures.

Reliable Communication

As we have seen, a key role for the peacemaker is to foster communication. The peacemaker must encourage and ensure that the parties accept—not necessarily agree with—the feelings and views expressed. This is essential to an understanding of the differences. The peacemaker must ensure that the parties listen to each other (see page 146). It is helpful to get each party to try to describe the position of the other—a form of role reversal.

In conflict, because the parties are working out of assumptions and stereotypes, one of the biggest barriers is the information filter each person uses to hear only what he wants to hear. The peacemaker must repeatedly check that the parties are hearing one another correctly. Ask them what they have heard before they respond. The use of a flip chart to list areas of difference and common ground is also helpful. Summarising helps tremendously to keep the parties focused on where they really are and what they are actually hearing.

PRODUCTIVE TENSION

If the parties are too relaxed, there will be little incentive to resolve their differences. On the other hand if the parties are under too much stress, they will become rigid, fixed and totally unable to explore new ways forward. We can illustrate this tension:

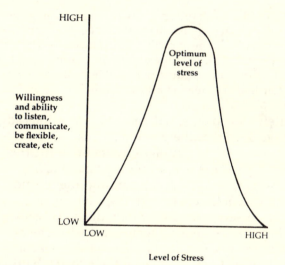

Level of Stress

At low levels of stress, there is no sense of urgency, no necessity to look for alternative ways of behaving, and no perceived need for reconciliation. At very high levels of stress, the threats and risks are so great that fear tends to immobilise the parties.

In his book *Pressure Points*, Pete Meadows offers some useful suggestions for those in the church who are suffering from stress. The principles he outlines are applicable in all

fields, especially his chapter entitled 'The Good Stressman-
ship Guide'. In this chapter, Meadows outlines in a
tongue-in-cheek manner (but actually very seriously) ways
in which we can add stress to others' lives:

> When faced with someone debilitated through stress, always
> ask 'What can I do?'.... Those swamped by stress are generally
> unable to make practical suggestions as to how others can
> come to their aid.... Never arrive on their doorstep to
> announce 'I've come for your ironing' or 'We would like to
> take the children for the day'.... This would be thoroughly
> counter-productive to the task in hand—it could actually
> relieve stress.

In the same chapter Meadows shows how we can also
add to the stress of groups with whom we are working:

> Make sure that each group is always kept just large enough so
> that real intimacy is unable to take place. A group of less than
> twelve will always be at risk in this connection. The leadership
> of the group must set an example in maintaining a level of
> superficiality and avoiding personal honesty; while the group
> must hardly ever meet on a social basis.[5]

Fortunately, few people will follow his facetious advice!
We have seen that the peacemaker can alter the levels of
stress in a way that encourages reconciliation. Stress can be
increased by leaving the parties together, locking the door,
raising sensitive issues, reminding the parties of the
consequences of failure and giving adverse, negative feedback. Conversely, stress may be reduced by breaks in the
discussions, prayer, encouragement, positive feedback, etc.
By these means, confrontation can lead to reconciliation.
Let us look now in more detail at the role of the third party,
the peacemaker in the whole process.

Acting as a Peacemaker

The peacemaker has three main roles, one in each of the
following areas: preparation for reconciliation, the reconciliation meeting itself, and follow-up to reconciliation.

PREPARATION FOR RECONCILIATION

To walk out on to the battlefield waving that white flag or carrying that round table is to risk becoming a target for both sides. Preparation is needed so that the peacemaker gains acceptance. Preparation also tests the readiness of the opponents for peace and enables the peacemaker to consider how best to structure the reconciliation. Questions such as who should be at the meeting? how many should represent each side? on what level should they be? what will be on the agenda? which topics will be raised first? who will speak first, for how long and according to what rules?—all must be answered before the process commences. These questions may in fact be the first items on the agenda, and others follow: where will the meeting be? whose territory is safe? is there a neutral location? how formal should the event be? should we sit at a table or in easy chairs or even not sit at all but go for a game of golf or a walk together? when should it be—morning, afternoon or evening—and how long should the first meeting last? should we plan more than one meeting? should the meeting be in stages? what will be the peacemaker's role? Before the initial reconciliation discussion can get under way, these questions too must be answered. It is the role of the peacemaker to clarify everything in advance.

THE RECONCILIATION MEETING

Depending on the role agreed for the peacemaker, he or she needs to ensure that the basic processes of reconciliation do take place: sharing, confessing, repenting and forgiving—either by initiating and controlling them himself, or by prompting the parties to take initiative. Here are some of the steps the peacemaker may usefully take:

1 *Referee the process.* This can be done by setting boundaries to acceptable behaviour and drawing attention to unconstructive positions or exchanges.

2 *Decide the agenda.* The peacemaker can suggest the course and the content of the meeting, probably in the early stages of the process. A clear agenda also helps to regulate the level of stress.

3 *Summarise*. This is very helpful. Simply and regularly sum up where the discussions have got to. This practice helps communication and gives the parties an overview of the process.

4 *Encourage openness*. Ask how people feel about situations, statements and attitudes. Give them an opportunity to express their views openly. Let them know that what they feel is important, and it is right and proper that they should share it and trust the other to keep the information confidential.

5 *Give feedback*. Tell the parties how you, as the peace-maker, see them—their behaviour, their attitudes, their reactions. Help them into the 'here and now' rather than staying in the 'then and there'.

6 *Keep the process clear*. Ensure that the two phases of differentiation and integration are fully dealt with and that the discussion does not swing back and forth.

7 *Assist with the diagnosis* of the sources of the conflict.

8 *Watch for communication failures*. Ask parties to repeat what the other has said and keep checking for understanding.

9 *Offer advice* and counsel as needed.

10 *Help focus* on the future.

ATMOSPHERE

The peacemaker needs to develop a high level of sensitivity, not only to his own emotional state, but to the emotional condition of others. How fast can the process move forward? When do the parties need to be confronted with unconstructive behaviour? When do the barriers need to come down, and when is it vital that the barriers remain in position? These questions lie at the heart of the converging process.

How sensitive are we to atmosphere? Can we walk into an office, a kitchen, a church and 'sense' the mood of the people there? Do we arrange the furniture in a room to give it a warm, protective atmosphere or instead create a challenging and threatening layout?

The symbolism of negotiation is significant. Have you noticed how international peace talks or industrial disputes progress? Often the opposing parties will begin in different cities with negotiators shuttling between the two. Henry Kissinger was the master of the 'shuttle diplomacy', as it came to be called. With progress, the delegations can move to one neutral city, but of course parties will occupy different hotels. With more progress a move to a third hotel— again neutral—becomes possible, then one conference room—but with different tables of course—and then eventually the agreement is signed with both parties side by side at the same table. Thus, in interpersonal peace-making, the peacemaker needs a high degree of sensitivity to atmosphere to decide the location, timing and layout of initiatives.

SEATING ARRANGEMENTS FOR PEACEMAKING

Phase One (Disengagement)

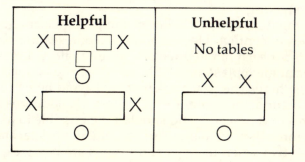

Putting both parties side by side at too early a phase will cause aggression to surface before it can be dealt with positively.

Phase Two (Convergence)

Helpful	Unhelpful
X ☐ X O	Use of long tables

The physical proximity of the parties is important. The closer together, but still with the security of the table, the better.

Phase Three (Integration)

Helpful	Unhelpful
X ^O X XO X	Use of any tables

Removal of all barriers between the parties and the coming together of mind and heart are the aims of phase three peacemaking.

In the diagrams, O indicates the peacemaker and X the parties in conflict. Helpful and unhelpful seating arrangements for each of the three phases are indicated. A square or rectangle represents a table, which is often critical to the atmosphere. The peacemaker should avoid being the only one behind the table. Certain rooms or locations are in themselves peaceful, and should it be possible to use such locations, they are particularly helpful in the later stages of phase two when feelings and futures are being explored. And in phase three, physical contact between the parties— sitting shoulder to shoulder, face to face with the opportunity for hands or knees to touch—will help the progress.

A Symbol of Peace

Reconciliation is a significant event. Its achievement should be marked by a celebration gift or act of symbolism. The church takes Christ's cross for its symbol, and the Communion (Eucharist or Lord's Supper) as the celebration of the reconciliation achieved by his death. Some churches give a sign of peace as part of their celebrations—a handshake, an embrace, a kiss—given by the members of the congregation to each other as a symbolic gesture of their peace and unity in Christ.

The peacemaker should choose for the reconciled parties some symbolic act of reconciliation. It may be an embrace, or the exchange of letters or gifts; it might be a rededication of the marriage vows; it may be the signing of a statement, a special photograph, meal, holiday, certificate, poem, quotation or verse from the Bible or other religious text. Whatever it is, this symbol belongs specially to the people, place and process of reconciliation — it is their own symbol of peace.

FOLLOW-UP

Continuing support is needed following conflict and reconciliation. Where possible, other skilled parties interested in helping the reconciliation should be encouraged to give support, provided they understand the background and aims of the process. Follow-up meetings with the peacemaker should be arranged. If the peacemaker is not readily available, it is useful to have another skilled peacemaker on hand to help with any on-going difficulties. What kind of person can fulfil this role? What are the attributes of the peacemaker?

The Peacemaker's Skills

Sadly, peacemakers are few and far between. One of the reasons we are so ineffective as peacemakers is that we have failed to take the trouble to develop the gifts and skills necessary to apply the principles of peace — even though we all know them. We therefore need the following capabilities, both in reality and in others' perception.

1   A recognition of the roots of conflicts
2   A sensitivity to feelings and atmosphere
3   The interpersonal skills needed to confront people and their behaviour
4   Creative ways out of impasses and repetitive behaviour
5   An acceptance of people whether we agree with their positions or not

6   The provision of emotional support and reassurance to people in distress

7   Good communication

8   No real power over the parties. If a peacemaker does have power—for example when the boss tries to act as peacemaker for members of his team—then the parties may tend to act only to please the power figure, rather than to resolve the conflict.

9   A degree of knowledge of the situation. The peacemaker must be known to be someone who understands the context of the conflict, whether church, school or business. Too detailed a knowledge, however, can be a disadvantage, for the parties are unlikely to believe that the peacemaker is unbiassed.

10   Neutrality. The peacemaker must not have any vested interest in either party, in the outcome, in the way he relates to either party, or in the ground rules or approaches used. If the peacemaker *is* biassed in any way, he will soon lose the trust of one or both parties.

11   Integrity and confidentiality. Disclosures may be made in the course of a reconciliation which if shared outside the context of a confidential supportive atmosphere could be destructive.

Risks for the Peacemaker

I have emphasised throughout this book that conflict is a dangerous pastime, hurtful not only to those involved, but to observers, and to potential peacemakers who often carry the burden of the cost. We have the supreme example of sacrificial peacemaking in the work of Jesus Christ.

Emotionally, spiritually and physically there are risks. There are other dangers, too, for the peacemaker: rejection by the parties, burnout, and entanglement in the conflict are potential hazards. In order to cope with these risks we should ensure that:

1   We have our own support network.

2   We keep our own inner peace through prayer, meditation and confession.

3   We remain true to ourselves and do not allow ourselves to become fixed in a role.

4   We take time to relax and restore our energies after a session with conflicting parties.
5   We limit our involvement with the parties and ensure that the conflict does not spill over into other areas of our life—family, work, church or leisure.
6   We keep check of our own stress levels.

Summary and Assessment

Peacemaking is a blessed activity, yet it is followed in Jesus' teaching by persecution, insult and false accusation.[6] Are we ready for it?

In my work I have met many who claimed to be in the business of peacemaking. I have met none who claimed 100 per cent success. I know a few who claim more than 50 per cent success. Most would agree that the usual outcome of conflict is more conflict; that is one of the burdens they have to bear. As I have searched for what characterises successful peacemaking, I have come across a number of factors that peacemakers report as vital. The following list contains fifteen of these. I have met no one who has them all, but the more we have, the more successful we are likely to be.

Rate Yourself as a Peacemaker

Score yourself against the following characteristics, circling the number on the scale that best reflects your own position, habits and attitudes.

1   I tend to hide my feelings.

Never					Always
10	8	6	4	2	0

2   I am embarrassed when people show emotion.

Never					Always
10	8	6	4	2	0

3   People respect me.

Always					Never
10	8	6	4	2	0

4   Prayer or meditation is a feature of my daily life.

Always					Never
10	8	6	4	2	0

5   I am persistent.

Always					Never
10	8	6	4	2	0

6   I am a good organiser.

Always					Never
10	8	6	4	2	0

7   I communicate well.

Always					Never
10	8	6	4	2	0

8   I am a good listener.

Always					Never
10	8	6	4	2	0

9   I am sensitive to atmosphere.

Always					Never
10	8	6	4	2	0

10   I am a support to others.

Always					Never
10	8	6	4	2	0

11   I relate well to people.

Always					Never
10	8	6	4	2	0

12 I can keep confidences.

Always					Never
10	8	6	4	2	0

13 I share problems with close colleagues.

Always					Never
10	8	6	4	2	0

14 I sleep well.

Always					Never
10	8	6	4	2	0

15 I can relax when I need to.

Always					Never
10	8	6	4	2	0

What is your total score? Whatever you score, you need to be better, but if you scored less than 100, it is not likely that you are ready for serious peacemaking. Start concentrating on those behaviours where you scored 6 or less.

CHAPTER ELEVEN

INNER PEACE

Whatever is pure, whatever is lovely, whatever is admirable
—if anything is excellent or praiseworthy—think about such
things.... And the peace of God will be with you.[1]

I N CHAPTER TEN we saw that it is important for the
peacemaker to have his or her own means for remain-
ing at peace. When we act as reconcilers, we are asso-
ciating with people whose own inner peace has gone,
whose interpersonal relationships are in a state of war. It is
difficult to switch off from such encounters, particularly if
the conflict has escalated towards mutual destruction. The
things said (or shouted) stay in our minds: they niggle at
us, rankle, and eat into our sleeping hours—unless we
adopt the techniques described in the previous chapter.

If we are familiar with these symptoms of a loss of inner
peace, then we will be able to appreciate something of the
problems faced by the parties in conflict. Of course, some
people are more thick-skinned than others: they even enjoy
a conflict or can shut it out of their minds. This chapter,
then, is to help us deal with the more sensitive client—the
person whose inner peace has been so deeply disturbed
that all their relationships are affected.

Restoring inner peace follows much the same process as
dealing with external forms of conflict. There are at least
eight steps on the road to the restoration of inner peace.

1 Establishing the facts and feelings.
2 Uncovering the framework of thoughts and behaviours.
3 Bringing to light the aims and motives and values which lie at the heart of the situation.
4 Coming to terms with the situation as it is.
5 Creating a new vision for inner peace.
6 Developing strategies to pursue the vision.
7 Encouraging and taking action.
8 Reviewing and maintaining the inner peace.

The following case illustrates these steps in relation to one man whose inner peace was broken because he found his aims frustrated.

Jack and Sylvia

It was Jack's wife who made the first move. She phoned my office and made an appointment to see me on 'a personal matter'. Jack and Sylvia had been married for fifteen years. Now both in their late thirties, they were a fairly normal executive family—two children, two cars, two holidays, and two dogs. Their two boys were doing well at school; their mortgage was low, and they had no health worries. So what was the problem?

'It's Jack, you see,' Sylvia struggled to explain. 'He's changed. I can't put my finger on it, but he's different, and it's affecting the whole family now. I can't explain it, and I don't know how to help him. Would you talk to him?'

Jack and Sylvia both worked for the same company to which I was contracted as a part-time counsellor. I talked with Sylvia for a while and gathered as much information as I could, taking notes and checking with her what I had written. There is a difference of opinion among counsellors as to whether one takes notes during sessions with clients. Since it is important to make notes of any reconciliation process, I prefer initially to make notes in front of the parties. This helps them come to terms with my role; it gives them a sense of confidence that the peacemaker is listening; and it also gives them time to think—I write more slowly than most people can talk!

Jack's problem was not with Sylvia. Jack had changed

towards everyone—the children, the dogs, his friends, his church and his colleagues at work.

Reconciliation is like a 'who dunnit?'. First, the peace-maker needs to establish the reason for the broken peace. It is a case of asking the what? when? where? and how? of the conflict. It is unlikely that the parties will be able to describe the 'why?' initially. They may have their views about why the conflict has developed, but my experience suggests that their perceptions are rarely accurate since the source of all conflict is internal and therefore often hidden from others.

'What has changed?' I asked. Sylvia was typical of a person caught up in a conflict with someone close to her, and she found it very difficult to be objective. In such situations I find the following question very useful. 'Tell me what he is doing more of and what he is doing less of?'

This question worked for Sylvia. She immediately launched into a long list of Jack's changed behaviour, which included spending a lot of time alone, staying late at the office when Sylvia knew the department was not busy, and—the behaviour that gave her the most concern—Jack had stopped going to church, something the family had always done together since the children were born.

The timing of the first signs of conflict is important. When did Sylvia first notice any changes? Jack had begun to excuse himself from church, where he had been heavily involved in installing a computer (this, to Sylvia, was the most obvious event) shortly after the new minister had arrived. Relationships had got steadily worse, in that Jack spent less and less time with the family. More questioning revealed that Jack was also seeing less and less of his friends, squash partners and the like.

What were Sylvia's reactions? She had tried to encourage Jack to talk about what was happening. At first she had expressed concern about his absence from church. Then as his withdrawal continued, she had got angry and they had fought over it. She had suggested that they go to another church, but he refused to consider that. The same pattern of concern, anger and confrontation had occurred over Jack's long office hours, and the reaction had been the same—excuses, apologies, confrontations, then a refusal to discuss it. At home Jack was withdrawn, uncommunicative and very different from the Jack of three years before.

It is essential in any peacemaking that the peacemaker establish his role, and that the expectations be understood and agreed. The peacemaker should primarily be a facilitator and is not there to arbitrate, negotiate or take up the cause of either party. Often, the peacemaker will be approached by parties who have totally unrealistic expectations of his role. 'Will you talk to him and make him see reason? He won't listen to me!' But the peacemaker must be clear and direct in his response to such requests—the answer must always be 'No!'

My initial reading of the situation between Jack and Sylvia was that the roots of the conflict did not lie in their relationship. Their deteriorating family life was simply, if tragically, an offshoot of something deeper. It seemed to me that Sylvia and Jack were suffering from some unresolved inner conflict with which Jack was struggling, but what had triggered the problem?

Faced with a Sylvia, the peacemaker has to make a fundamental choice in his initial strategy. Do I seek to make contact with the other party at the earliest opportunity, or do I seek to work into that situation through the one party who has taken the initiative and come to me? Since the root of the problem seemed to be in Jack and not in the relationship itself, I opted to make contact with Jack, but how? Simple, direct and open approaches are the most successful in reconciliation, so the choice was either for me to make direct contact with Jack and explain that Sylvia had been to see me, or for Sylvia to tell Jack about our 'discussion'. Though I had met Jack on several occasions at lunches and work events so that a direct contact from me would not have caused problems, I decided that it would be much better if the initiator, in this case Sylvia, made the link. This she did, and Jack came to see me the following week.

The Presenting Problem

The fact that he came at all indicated a willingness to talk, and the fact that he had come so soon after Sylvia's visit indicated a sense of urgency. After the initial welcomes and preliminaries to help him feel at ease, I took the initiative by explaining what my role was and what I hoped from the meeting. For the first I would be a listener, interpreter and joint explorer of Jack's concerns. For the second I hoped that in the hour together we could establish a partnership which would enable Jack to make some decisions about his relationships. I explained that, should Jack wish it, I would make myself available for four follow-up meetings.

I then gave Jack the opportunity to ask some questions about me and the process that I would use. He was particularly concerned about confidentiality and note-taking. 'In situations like this,' I explained, 'the notes I take belong to the client. At the end of our session we will run through the notes I have made and you will take them with you. If you come back for any further discussions you should bring the file with you, and we'll begin by reading over the notes of the previous session.'

This put his mind at rest, so he sat back and with a nervous smile said, 'Well, where do we begin?' Jack was intelligent and articulate, and he needed little help in sharing the facts. He had been disappointed when the new minister had 'taken over' the development of the church computer, on which Jack had been working for almost two years. 'He clearly thought he could do it better than I— so I let him,' Jack explained.

'You had put a lot of effort into its development?' I asked.

'Several hundred hours, I guess. It was quite sophisticated—covered finance, maintenance, membership, visitation, skills and resources of members, library and a five-year planning system. It was the planning system that was taking the time. As far as I know there isn't one in the country yet.'

'And...' I encouraged.

'And—well—the new guy just didn't appreciate it. Said he had used a computer in his last place to produce his sermons and didn't need any help. What he meant was he had used a word processor, not a computer.' Jack then declared with some anger, 'He obviously didn't value my work.'

'How did you feel about that?' was my next question.

'Well, that was it.' Jack shrugged his shoulders. 'If he didn't want me, then I didn't need him. So I stopped going.'

I made a few notes to give Jack some space and time for reflection, then I asked, 'What about Sylvia?'

'Oh, she thinks he's great and can't understand why I won't go any more!'

'And have you told her why you won't go?'

Jack hesitated. 'Well, no, not really I suppose. I mean we've talked about it, of course.'

'Talked about what?' I probed.

'About not going to church,' Jack retorted.

'Not about the computer?' I pressed.

'Sylvia doesn't understand computers. She's not interested.'

'Do you miss going to church?' I asked, to move the focus back on to Jack.

'Yes, I suppose I do. It was something we did as family, and I felt recognised and appreciated before this new minister came.'

'Family is important to you then?'

'Yes, of course.'

'And recognition?'

He hesitated, then smiled, 'Yes, that too. I hadn't thought of it that way, but yes. The computer project gave me the chance to do something that no one else could do. Without that there was no sense of achievement for me.'

We talked for another fifteen minutes. Jack was a man of high personal and professional standards. He was achievement orientated. Bereft of his pioneering project at church, Jack had thrown himself into his work to try to meet the needs of his inner desire for achievement.

Achievement motivation is one of the three primary social motives described by Professor David McClelland.[2] People with high achievement needs seek:

— continued high performance
— moderately challenging task
— to improve their standards
— feedback on how they are doing
— freedom to work at their own speed.

With the loss of his church computer project Jack had ceased to experience a sense of motivation in the church and had therefore sought satisfaction elsewhere.

I shared my notes with Jack, then offered to look deeper if he wanted to come back. I knew by the way the latter part of the discussion had gone that he would accept.

In this first session with Jack I had been able to encourage him to articulate the facts as he saw them, his feelings and his aims and motives. Some more work was needed on this last aspect before he could go on to explore some of his deeper values and beliefs. Jack had used two key phrases, which I had written down for him: 'He obviously didn't value my work' and 'If he didn't want me, then I didn't need him.'

As an achiever, Jack associated worth with doing rather than being. For Jack, people were valued for what they do rather than what they are. Thus the minister's rejection of Jack's work was the same to Jack as rejecting Jack himself. (Reference to the diagram on page 56 will show that Jack was suffering from loss of self-esteem, denial, avoidance and withdrawal.) Rather than confront the situation, Jack had stepped into the cycle of hurt, page 50.

Motivation

McClelland's work on motivation identified three 'primary social motives'.[3] These are inner drives which to a large extent influence our behaviour. The three primary social motives are the need for achievement, the need for affiliation, and the need for power and influence.

Whereas affiliators have a great desire to be with others and gain satisfaction from belonging to groups, teams, clubs and societies, an achiever is happy to work alone. Meanwhile, the individual whose primary social motive is power has a strong desire to influence people and situations. Such people usually make good leaders or managers. A mixture of high achievement and high power motivation is quite common in leaders. (Those interested in the subject of motivation should read *Power, the Inner Experience*,[4] which treats the subject in depth.)

Jack was strongly achievement oriented, low in affiliation and only partly motivated by a desire for power. We talked about these findings and now began to explore Jack's values. What was important to him? What did he want to do with his life? What kind of people and situations did he value? These are key questions when dealing with inner conflict since they open the way to an examination of a person's beliefs about himself and his world.

When Jack returned for his second session, we reviewed the notes (which, by the way, he had shared with Sylvia— a significant step since he was now being more open).

Irrationality

Most people carry around a set of beliefs which are not rational, born of unrealistic expectations of ourselves and others. We build a false picture of the world and espouse beliefs that are untenable under examination. In fact few people ever bother to examine their beliefs fully. One writer on the subject[5] has identified a number of false beliefs common in Western society, and I am indebted to John Lightbody of the Seven Sisters project in Liverpool for the following summary of the ten most common irrational beliefs. Check how many you agree with— we are all somewhat irrational!

1   It is necessary for an adult to have the love, approval and respect of all those around them.
2   An adult should be perfect in all he undertakes.
3   The world is made up of good and evil people. The evil should be punished.
4   It is bad when things are not entirely how I would like them to be.
5   External events are the major cause of human unhappiness.
6   The world we inhabit is a risky place full of danger to the unwary.
7   Unpleasant tasks are to be avoided.
8   Everyone needs something or someone stronger than himself to rely on.
9   The future is determined by the past.
10   Things are getting better if only we don't interfere. So don't rock the boat.

For Jack, the desire for approval and perfection, and the conviction of unhappiness stemming from external causes lay at the root of his inner conflict. We shared this list at our third meeting and began to explore where and why Jack might have developed these beliefs.

His need for approval and perfection were the products of high achieving, demanding parents. His inability to achieve either approval or perfection had led him to project the source of his unhappiness on the world which denied him success.

Jack's willingness to explore the contents of the sessions with Sylvia was a great help to him. By his fourth visit, he came with a plan prepared to visit the vicar—who was still only using the computer as a word processor—and to share with him his vision of an advanced computer programme which would assist the church in its goals. Jack was also prepared to be open about his feelings (confession), to acknowledge that his behaviour had been wrong (repentance) and to ask for the opportunity to rebuild his relationships in the church.

Jack had first to come to terms with himself. Although he had taken offence at the vicar's attitude (which I agree was at fault—it always takes two!), it was Jack's own irrational beliefs which had destroyed his peace and satisfaction. He had come to realise that his value to others goes deeper than simply what he could do. Jack's church now has Jack back, and three years later it also has what is probably the most advanced long-range planning system in any church in Britain!

Motivation Questionnaire

One of the tools that I used to help Jack come to terms with his own motivation follows. You may like to try it yourself to understand better what impels you as you think and act at home and in your job.

SCORING INSTRUCTIONS

Read each of the statements and score yourself 3 points if you often behave that way, 2 points if you sometimes behave in that way, and no points if you rarely or never behave in that way. Note that this questionnaire is difficult to answer objectively. It is helpful to remember that there are no 'right' or 'wrong' answers—only accurate and inaccurate ones! So try to be as honest with yourself as you can.

Score

SET A

1	I like to do the best I can.	_____
2	I enjoy doing new things.	_____
3	I like to take part in competitive sports.	_____
4	I dream of achieving great things.	_____
5	I try to improve on my past performances.	_____
6	I like to have clear goals.	_____
7	I enjoy taking moderate risks.	_____
8	I like to know how well I am doing.	_____
9	I prefer to work on my own.	_____
10	I set myself high personal standards.	_____
11	I let folk know when they have done a good job.	_____
12	I tend to compare people's performances.	_____
13	Given a task, I tend to plan it carefully.	_____
14	I find rules and regulations restricting.	_____
15	I enjoy success.	_____

Total A _____

SET B

16	I like to make new friends.	_____
17	I am a co-operative person.	_____
18	I like organising get-togethers.	_____
19	People are more important to me than performance.	_____
20	I keep in touch with old friends.	_____
21	I am sensitive to people's feelings.	_____
22	I am easily hurt.	_____
23	I tend to say what I think people want to hear.	_____
24	I like to work in teams.	_____
25	I praise other people's efforts.	_____
26	I enjoy sharing with people.	_____
27	Relationships are important to me.	_____
28	I avoid conflict whenever possible.	_____
29	I have a wide circle of friends.	_____
30	I am a compassionate person.	_____

Total B _____

SET C

31	I enjoy influencing others.	_____
32	Reputation is important to me.	_____
33	I enjoy giving instructions to others.	_____
34	I am regarded as an outspoken person.	_____
35	I am status conscious.	_____
36	I enjoy a good argument.	_____
37	I like to bargain.	_____
38	I like to make decisions.	_____
39	I find information helps one to influence people.	_____
40	I am good at getting people to do what I want.	_____
41	Change excites me.	_____
42	I enjoy coaching people.	_____
43	I collect things.	_____
44	Possessions matter to me.	_____
45	I like to encourage younger people.	_____

Total C _____

RESULTS

The three sets A, B and C relate to the three primary social motives, achievement, affiliation and power. There is nothing intrinsically good or bad about strength or weakness in any of the three motives, but your strengths and weaknesses will affect your behaviour as a peacemaker. The table on page 184 shows the possible effects of your primary social motives on your approaches to reconciliation. Scores over 35 on any motive should be regarded as high; below 25 as low.

Summary

The roots of all conflict are within us. No matter what the presenting problems, no matter how far the conflict has escalated and how many people have been drawn into it, the heart of the strife is the heart of man. Inner peace is the greatest prize for peacemakers. Without it, interpersonal conflict will develop. In Jack and Sylvia's case both were willing to seek peace, but what should the peacemaker do when one party—or both—is set on victory? Let us now examine the approach when *aggression* rules.

PRIMARY SOCIAL MOTIVE	POSSIBLE IMPLICATIONS FOR PEACEMAKING ACTIVITIES	
	HIGH IN MOTIVE	LOW IN MOTIVE
ACHIEVEMENT	1 May push too hard, too soon. 2 May tend to take sides. 3 May be too impatient.	1 May be satisfied with a low quality peace. 2 May not demand enough of the parties. 3 May not give enough feed-back to the parties.
AFFILIATION	1 May be too willing to compromise. 2 May be unable to give negative feed-back. 3 May be unwilling to take the initiative.	1 May be insensitive to parties' feelings. 2 May be unable to sustain close relationships with parties over long periods. 3 May be unable to work with other peacemakers as a team.
POWER	1 May tend to encourage a nego-tiated settlement. 2 May tend to domi-nate the process and so come between the parties. 3 Parties may agree, just to please the peacemaker.	1 May lack authority. 2 May allow the process to be domi-nated by one or other of the parties. 3 May be unwilling to confront the parties with their negative behaviour.

CHAPTER TWELVE

DEALING WITH AGGRESSION

"Nearly everybody enjoys it," he added. "It's a pretty useful job. You get to work with nuclear weapons. You get to work with the most sophisticated intercontinental ballistic missiles in the world. It's accurate and it works first time every time. I've been working with missiles for ten years and I've enjoyed it—it's a lot of fun."

Peacemaker missile control officer[1]

T HIS ASTOUNDING PARAGRAPH from a professional soldier reminds us that, for some people, conflict is a way of life. But those who enjoy conflict are not confined to missile managers.

Recently I consulted with a man who lived for conflict. At work he would take every opportunity to exercise his aggression. He would publicly attack his staff, undermine his superiors and provoke his colleagues whenever he could. His home life was not much different. At work his fellow employees tended to excuse his behaviour on the basis of the supposition that his family life was in trouble, while at home his wife would explain to the children, 'Dad has had a bad day at the office!'

In the course of my dealings with this one-man civil-war, I uncovered a very deep sense of anger and disappointment. He felt unfulfilled, unrecognised and undervalued. His aggression was his way of making an impact on his world.

Despite his undoubted intelligence and ability, he had put most of his energy into learning and practising the skills of interpersonal conflict.

In this chapter I want to discover some tools to help us deal with the approaches to conflict described in Chapter Four. In fact, there are a number of features of conflict we must be able to identify before we can choose an appropriate strategy. The key features are, as we have already seen:

1 The scale of conflict, as described in Chapter One.
2 The level to which the conflict has escalated, which we dealt with in Chapter Two.
3 The cause of the conflict, which we examined in Chapter Three.
4 The approach being adopted—Chapter Four.

In addition to these, we need to learn to understand something of the parties involved and of ourselves as potential peacemakers. But first let us consider some of the common behaviours used. These correspond to eight of the nine attitudes on page 78. Reconciliation, the ninth, is treated in relation to all eight.

Behaviours

Faced with opposition, a determined individual will adopt preferred behaviour. It will be 'preferred' usually because it has worked before. The more we use a particular approach, the more skilled we become at it, although the choice of behaviour will also be influenced by the situation and the opposition. The approaches to conflict matrix, page 79, show the nine approaches most commonly adopted in conflict. It is important for any would-be peacemaker to know the behaviour associated with these approaches, to be able to recognise them in use and—if necessary—to use them if the focus of the conflict should bring the peacemaker under attack from one or both the conflicting parties.

COLLABORATIVE BEHAVIOUR

As we have seen, only reconciliation offers real peace—all other approaches are 'preparation for war'. But the time for reconciliation may not be right. There is a time for every purpose, but there is also a *place* for every purpose. Sir Isaac Newton said, 'Give me a place to stand and I will move the earth.' He was considering the power of leverage —if you have a long enough lever you can move mountains. In conflict, the same principle applies; it is possible to defeat the enemy if you are in the right position, no matter how strong the opposition.

From the collaborator's viewpoint, the time is not right to attack—the enemy is too strong, so the collaborator bides his time and seeks to strengthen his position. He does this by deliberately positioning himself.

Positioning requires the collaborator to do three things:

—locate the enemy's weak points
—close in on the enemy, and
—attempt to destroy the enemy when the time is right.

A graphic example of positioning is to be found in one of the lesser-known books of the Old Testament, the Book of Esther, named after the Jewish wife of Xerxes I, the Persian king from 486 to 465 BC. A plot is uncovered in which a leading politician urges genocide of the Jews in the kingdom. The enemy is located, but he is powerful. How can he be destroyed?

The queen prepares an elaborate plan. She gains the favour of the king and makes two requests: first that the king and Haman—the villain of the story—come to a feast that she has prepared (step two—close in on the enemy); then that they come again a second day since the party has been a great success. Haman is now completely off guard. The record states that after the first day of feasting, 'Haman went out that day happy and in high spirits'.[2] On the second day, choosing her time with great skill, Queen Esther exposes the plot against her people. The king is now only too ready to have the politician and his supporters executed.

The account illustrates the first of the classic conflict

behaviours. Positioning is extremely effective (though it cannot lead to reconciliation) since it tends to be surreptitious, and the positioning party may only declare his position when it is too late for the other party to react effectively in defence or evade the attack.

For the peacemaker, a conflict in which one party is using collaborative behaviour is one of the most difficult with which to deal. Faced with this kind of approach the only route open to the peacemaker is to attempt to prevent the parties from coming together until there is mutual commitment to reconciliation. Beware of what appears to be a progressive coming together of the parties, but is no more than an attempt by one party to get the other to drop its guard long enough to deal a disabling or fatal blow.

Do not therefore attempt to bring about reconciliation unless you know the position and intention of the opposing forces. Sit down and count the cost with each party of going to war—it is always too much to pay. Finally, discernment is needed to ensure that we are not used to set up a situation that gives unfair advantage to one party.

AVOIDANCE BEHAVIOUR

Conflicts can become protracted, debilitating experiences when one or both parties avoid confrontation yet maintain hostilities. This may seem, on the surface, a good thing, but it will increase the frustration and the bitterness of the parties and make reconciliation much more difficult. The reasons for avoidance are usually to do with timing, strength or values. One party may assess the situation and conclude that the time for confrontation is not yet. Its members may wish to gather more support, more information, or wait for a particular time or place to face their opponent. A more confused rationale may have to do with non-violent values; for example, one party may not hold with or be able to cope with conflict and therefore seek to deny it rather than face it in a non-violent way. In such conflicts a cat-and-mouse game develops in which one party hunts and pins down the other in order that the conflict may be resolved, while the mouse has no intention of being pinned down! A well-known avoidance story is the account of Israel's first king—King Saul—and his regular hunting of the shepherd David who was to become the second king.[3]

Avoidance is a recipe for growing frustration for someor.e who would rather have confrontation. The inability to resolve the situation face-to-face causes increasing desperation and growing conflict. This is the power of guerrilla warfare. The enemy are there; you know they are, but they will not stand and fight or play by the rules. Avoidance behaviour calls for a third party. The reconciler must work to understand fully the one who is avoiding the sharing of facts and feelings. The aim here is to strengthen the party that feels too weak to face the opposition.

DEFENSIVE BEHAVIOUR

In the face of an attack one party may attempt to sit tight and hope that the opposition will prove less determined than its own defences, for in essence that is what dictates the outcome of an entrenched position: the determination of the attacker. No structure, no position is impregnable —no bank, no vault is safe against the determined thief. In the first part of this century both the French and the Germans built large-scale defence systems—the Maginot and the Siegfried Lines—in attempts to make their positions secure. Both systems proved useless as means of defending their countries; the determined aggressor will find ways around, over, under or through any defence.

Entrenchment is only a temporary respite; it cannot be used for ever. Jerusalem fell to the determined Romans in AD 66; Troy fell; the Bastille fell; Vietnam fell; the Falkland Islands were retaken. Entrenchment is also a high-risk strategy; but it gives the defender a sense of security, however false it may be. Faced with an entrenched defender, the peacemaker may have great difficulty in persuading him that reconciliation is needed. 'Surely they will go away.' 'We can hold out indefinitely.' These are erroneous views that need to be changed.

COMPROMISING BEHAVIOUR

The temptation to settle differences through trade-offs is very high. It appeals to the rational, logical, thinking parts of our being. 'I can weigh this concession against that, and I agree to settle for second-best.' Compromise is the easiest of the assertive processes, but it carries with it the greatest hidden costs, since with neither party satisfied, both will continue to look for opportunities to pursue their real goals. Next time, however, because of the disappointment with an assertive approach, one or both parties is likely to become aggressive; the conflict thus escalates.

Persuading convicted compromisers that their approach is doomed is not easy. The reconciler will have more success if he follows two courses towards them. The first is to focus on the long-term perspective. Compromise is always based on where we are now rather than on where we want to be; so by pushing the parties to look at the future, the peace-maker can help them prepare plans to come together, rather than simply to agree to the slight modifications in their behaviour essential to compromise. The second strategy is based on creativity. Compromise is based on judging and evaluating what we have and where we are. Once again this focuses attention on the *differences* between us *now*. Reconciliation, however, is about what we might become, on what our common vision might be. (Chapter Six explored this theme.)

NEGOTIATIVE BEHAVIOUR

Negotiation is based on bargaining which focuses on the rightness of the parties. 'I have this; you have that.' 'So if I give you this, and you give me that, then...' — then you both lose! Reconciliation, however, focuses not on the rightness, but on the *wrongness* of the parties. Reconciliation begins by recognising what we have not got: we have not got right on our side; we are in the wrong; we are starting from a place of weakness, and that is no place from which to conduct a negotiation!

Faced with the would-be negotiator, the peacemaker should emphasise that since both parties are in the wrong, the only value of a negotiation is to trade one 'wrongness' for another. Bargaining is always a sign that the parties have not yet come to recognise the need for confession, repentance and forgiveness. It may be, of course, that the parties are not seeking reconciliation, but only a mutual, minimal loss of face. As a peacemaker you really must ask yourself if this is the business that you want to be in. Do not feel that you must be involved whatever the cost and whatever the parties wish. You will only end up devaluing the process, and yourself with it, if you let one or both of the parties dictate the terms and conditions under which you will be involved. If they want to negotiate after you have shown the inadequacy of negotiation, then withdraw and leave them to it. Reconciliation is too precious to waste on those who think it can be picked up cheaply in a back-street bargain. Urge parties, then, to opt for reconciliation rather than negotiation.

CONFRONTATIVE BEHAVIOUR

Confrontation is a form of aggression, yet it often precipitates peace. It is, however, high-risk. If one party is prone to confronting the other, the weaker party may repeatedly back off or become defensive. Alternatively, if the perceived power-base is equal, then both parties may get into a damaging 'head-banging' in which the immovable force meets the irresistible object. An impossible situation ensues in which great damage is done unless the peacemaker can more positively redirect the energies. This is the key to dealing with confrontation.

If the peacemaker does not act quickly, the process will go out of control. His first task is to slow down the frantic exchange of accusation and counter-accusation. He does this by summarising, clarifying and repeating statements. Thus we may intervene with 'Let me see if I understand what each of you is saying.' 'I don't think I understand that. I'll try to repeat it in my own words.'

Where more than one person is involved in each party, we may need a more formal approach. On a flip chart we can record our summaries, and the very act of writing things down causes the parties to hold off until they see that the written statements are correct. In this approach the mediator is very much in control; the results are dramatic, for the parties' behaviour is far less likely to degenerate into competition.

COMPETITIVE BEHAVIOUR

Competition is very common in conflict. The outcome desired is a win for one side and a lose for the other. In a competitive situation it is more effective to take the struggle to the enemy than allow the enemy to hold the initiative. There are five reasons for this:

1   It takes some time before the opposition is able to identify the initiator's intentions.
2   It gives the initiator the feeling of being in control.
3   It moves the initiator closer to his objectives.
4   Action will trigger a response and therefore will tend to bring the opposition out into the open in confrontation, thus hastening the conclusion.
5   Actions signal to the opposition a state of readiness and confidence, and this tends to lower the morale of the enemy.

Often the earlier the initiative, the greater the advantage, thus the pre-emptive strike can be a temptation to attempt to shorten the extent and reduce the damage of a conflict. This is one of the dangers for the peacemaker—the risk that one side will constantly try to get a few steps ahead in the conflict.

Once again we can illustrate this tactic from the Old Testament. As the children of Israel progressed in their conquest of the Promised Land, they came into the region occupied by the Gibeonites, who saw, with growing concern, their progress. The power and success of the Israelites was clearly a threat to the inhabitants of Gibeon. A small, unwarlike tribe, they could not hope to withstand the might of a million men. So the Gibeonites took the initiative. What they lacked in power, they made up in cunning. They arranged a treaty. A small group dressed themselves in travel-stained clothing and, feigning to come from a distant land, tricked the Israelites into an eternal peace treaty! When the deception was discovered, the Israelites felt forced to honour their commitment. By taking the initiative, the Gibeonites had gained the advantage.[4]

Again, the siege of the Iranian embassy in London showed to the world the effectiveness of regaining the initiative. On a much greater scale the D-day landings of World War II showed that a regained initiative can take the strongest of positions—though not without cost. But despite these examples of success, initiatives are usually high-risk, fraught with danger for the participants, as the following case illustrates.

John and Peter were brothers, both in their family business. John, the elder by four years, was quite happy to maintain the business on the lines that father had built up, whereas Peter—impetuous, competitive, creative and opportunistic—wanted to develop the enterprise into new areas. The brothers had never been close, and there was growing resentment in Peter; who felt that he was carrying the business but as junior partner had least say. In the year prior to my involvement, the partnership had been rocked by the 'discovery' that Peter was running two other businesses on the side—both of which had crashed, leaving considerable debts and a lot of bad feeling in their trade. Not content with these clandestine initiatives, Peter now was putting all his energies into making John's life a misery by pushing him out of the partnership.

This was the situation when their father called for help to sort out the relationship. But it was too late. Peter was a born competitor. In his attempts to get ahead and stay ahead, he had taken initiatives which resulted in criminal proceedings against the partnership. The business crashed. John emigrated and Peter was sentenced to three years for fraud.

In peacemaking, the peacemaker should always seek to control the process. On some occasions, the control will be taken from the peacemaker since surprise counter-attack may be used by one of the parties. We should be constantly on the alert for the counter-attack. When one comes, it usually only serves to escalate the conflict. Tit-for-tat spirals should be broken at the earliest opportunity. As peacemakers we should attempt to take and keep control as long as we can. If we lose it, we should take time to plan the next step to regain it. Reconciliation is very difficult if one of the conflicting parties continues to try to maintain the initiative.

Two relief organisations were attempting to co-operate on a joint project in Africa. One of the organisations was American, the other European. Problems had arisen over the style of management used. The American parent organisation gave a lot of freedom to its field managers, whereas the other organisation required the managers to report back weekly and to gain approval for all financial decisions.

Soon the two head offices were in quite serious conflict over how decisions in the field should be taken. The Americans, who were used to action in the field, also tried to take the initiative to solve the problem of the head office relationship. This initiative by the Americans was seen by the Europeans as being just typical high handedness! Throughout the reconciliation process which followed, the North American partners had to learn to exercise restraint, despite their enthusiasm for a settlement.

ATTACKING BEHAVIOUR

'Surprise is worth a thousand soldiers.' This view is not new. The early Jewish leader Gideon found that he could take on forces which were numerically hundreds of times his superior. Faced with an invading army of enormous proportions, he was guided to a great victory with only 300 men. The secret?—a night-time surprise attack with sufficient noise to confuse and disorientate the enemy. More damage was done to the opposition by its own men than by Gideon's attacking forces. The surprised opposition was caught off guard and forced into ill-considered reactions.[5]

The Israeli raid on Entebbe airport in Uganda after the hijack of an El-Al jet in 1976 is a modern example of the power of surprise. Flying 2,000 miles across hostile Africa, a group of commandos rescued 100 civilian hostages from the hands of determined and ruthless terrorists. No one expected a rescue attempt. Uganda seemed to be cooperating with the terrorists rather than trying to gain the hostages' release. The position looked hopeless, yet the raid surprised the terrorists, and the daring venture was a dramatic success, although three hostages were killed.

If one party believes that 'war' is inevitable, then a surprise attack is often seen as a very useful strategy. However, it requires careful planning. The failed American bid to rescue the embassy prisoners from Tehran illustrates how badly wrong surprise attacks can go.

Surprises can involve distance, timing and positioning. Often the greatest gains can be achieved by the combatant altering his normal behaviour. The usually quiet, gently-spoken Messiah used surprise tactics in the very stronghold of his opponents and drove the money-changers from the temple courts.[6]

For the peacemaker, a surprise attack by one party is often impossible to deal with. There are, however, two approaches that seem to reduce the impact and likelihood of surprise. First, we must get close to each side. This places a moral constraint on the parties. Second, we should seek some form of sanction to deter the parties from using surprise attacks. See also the ideas in the section on barriers to conflict, pages 113–117.

Keeping It Simple

Although we can describe on paper easily enough these eight approaches to conflict which do not result in reconciliation, in practice matters are of course more complicated. During a single reconciliation meeting, parties will engage in a great variety of behaviours. Perhaps they begin aggressively and then back off as they sense the strength of the peacemaker, or perhaps they start defensively, only to discover a chance to score a few points at the expense of the opposition. One lesson is important for the mediator: be ready for any behaviour. That means keeping our strategies simple and consolidating any movement towards reconciliation.

Murphy's law states that 'If anything can go wrong it will, unless you are prepared for it, in which case something else will go wrong!' In life and in relationships it is impossible to plan for every eventuality. Thus to attempt to consider all possible tactics of a conflict is of little value. Similarly, if a strategy to resolve a conflict is complex, it is less likely to be successful than a strategy which is basically simple.

The rescue bid in Iran relied heavily on helicopters — ten times more complex than the very basic Hercules transport planes used by the Israelis. The liberation of the Falkland Islands was successful in part because it was simple. Surprise was not possible; 8,000 miles of sea lay between Britain and the invaded islands. A direct, seaborne landing was decided upon; and, in the full knowledge of the world and the enemy, a straightforward approach won the day, but again, not without cost.

Joshua's attack on Jericho in the Old Testament was simplicity itself. Unskilled in siege warfare, the Israelites faced a daunting task with the walled fortress, but Joshua's strategy needed nothing more than obedience and patience.[7]

We should keep our reconciliation strategies free from encumbrances, making them as clean and streamlined as we can. In this way the risk of failure due to breakdowns in communication, planning or understanding will be minimised. In conflicts there is often so much mistrust that the parties have come to suspect not only the enemy but everyone else. I have found that a direct, face-to-face encounter is always to be preferred to a highly sophisticated, political or heavily structured approach with rules, regulations, meetings and more meetings about meetings.

CONSOLIDATING PROGRESS

Conflict weakens all those involved; even the supposed 'victor' suffers hurt during the encounters. It is therefore important in a sustained conflict that as peacemakers we take time to consolidate any progress towards reconciliation.

In warfare consolidation happens as troops dig in, bring up supplies and treat the injured. They also take time to ensure that morale is improved in readiness for the next offensive. In the context of reconciliation involving argument, debate and other exchanges, consolidation is no less important. If we can move the parties forward, we should attempt to secure the progress made—get it recorded, put it in writing, have it announced, agreed by the committees, deacons, management, etc—make it more difficult, in fact, for the parties to back down from the new position in the future, and take time to strengthen the morale of both sides before moving on to the next stage of reconciliation.

Jesus sent his disciples out into the villages to proclaim the kingdom of God and to do miracles, for a real spiritual battle was taking place (although it is doubtful if the disciples fully appreciated this). On their return, Christ commends them and takes them away for a few days to recover their strength.[8] Consolidation is important, particularly if the reconciliation process is protracted.

Summary

In this chapter I have tried to outline some of the methods by which the mediator can manage the behaviour of parties in conflict. You will find the behaviour that is closest to your *own* approach to conflict (see page 79) the most difficult to handle. Only practice improves our capacity to deal with those most like us.

Clearly, there is no single way to find reconciliation. Its processes are as varied as the faces that confront one another across the gulf of conflict.

CHAPTER THIRTEEN

PEACING TOGETHER

Will it be as before—
Peace, with no heart or mind to ensure it,
Guttering down to war
Like a libertine to his grave? We should not be surprised:
We knew it happen before.[1]

BETWEEN THE TOWNS of Berwick-upon-Tweed and Carlisle on the borders of England and Scotland lies a tribute to the Romans' attempts to maintain the peace of the outward reaches of their empire. Hadrian's Wall is a lasting, mocking symbol of a one-sided approach to peacemaking. Some 100 miles north of Hadrian's Wall lies Antoine's Wall, less known and less effective, but still visible after 2,000 years as another futile attempt at keeping the peace. Before the Romans, the Chinese did it with their Great Wall. After the Romans the Venetians did it around the Mediterannean. Then the East Germans did it with the Berlin Wall and the French with the Maginot Line in this century.

Walls may prevent war, but they do not keep peace. Peace is an attitude of mind and heart, and it does not develop in the shadow of a wall or defence system no matter how long, no matter how strategic. Walls cast shadows of fear. Defence does not make peace; it simply keeps war at bay—for a time. Yet no peace is for ever. The nature of human relationships is such that, at best, we will

experience conflict, reconciliation, conflict, reconciliation
— if we are fortunate.

Ownership

When I first began working in peacemaking I made many
mistakes and faced many disappointments and setbacks.
In particular I was frequently disheartened when I had
worked hard and long to bring parties together—success-
fully, so it seemed—only to receive a telephone call, letter
or visit which announced, 'It isn't working!' What had I
done wrong? What had I not done? Why had the reconciliation not lasted? Often I would have the chance to rework
the relationship, but even then there were times when the
new peace was again short-lived.

I had yet to learn just how fragile a new peace can often
be. True there were reconciliations which were profound
and persistent, yet it seemed that their making had followed
a similar pattern to the short-lived peaces. What made the
difference?

The difference was in the expectations of the parties. In
reconciliations which lasted, the parties recognised the
fragility of their peace. They recognised that if the peace
was broken, they were both responsible. In a word, the
difference was 'ownership'. They owned the relationship,
and they accepted responsibility for it. They both worked
hard at keeping the peace. They had learned what peacing
together meant.

Will it be as before?

I began the book with a look back at our history. How
better to end it than to look to tomorrow? It can be different
— for some it will be. Dear, persistent reader, you have
come a long way with me down the painful paths which are
the record of our own selfish ways. The journey is not over;
the destination is not determined; we can change and in
changing we can help others to change also. By beginning
to work at 'peacing' we can become a new force for reconciliation in our world.

Great are the dangers facing mankind. There are enough elements of confrontation, but the forces wishing and capable of stopping and overcoming that confrontation are growing in strength and scope before our very eyes.

Moving from suspicion and hostility to confidence, from a 'balance of fear' to a balance of reason and good will. . . . This is the goal of our peace initiative and for this we shall continue tirelessly to work.[2]

By working at it together, we can ensure that we keep our own peace and encourage those who would work with us to create longer lasting peaces. Then perhaps the ripples of your endeavours will join with mine so that our efforts at peacing together might rock this frail battleship, Earth, and tip its ballast more towards peace than conflict.

NOTES

Introduction

[1] Edward De Bono, *Conflicts* (Harrap: London, 1985), p 196.
[2] St Francis of Assisi, 'Prayer for Peace'; see also Matthew 5:9, 'Blessed are the peacemakers, for they will be called sons of God.'
[3] Matthew 5:11.
[4] *Seconds Away!* (MARC Europe: London, 1986), p 134.

Chapter One

[1] J R Miller, *The Every Day of Life* (Hodder and Stoughton: London, 1885), p 15.
[2] Ephesians 6:12.
[3] Isaiah 14:12–17.
[4] Ecclesiasticus 38:9,12–13.
[5] Francis Schaeffer and Everett Koop, *Whatever Happened to the Human Race?* (Marshall Morgan and Scott: London, 1980).
[6] *Faith in the City* (Church House Publishing: London, 1985).
[7] Genesis 13:11.
[8] *op cit.*
[9] Prof H M Conn, *Changing the World* (MARC Europe: Bromley 1988) p 33.
[10] See Isaiah 9:6–7.
[11] Frank Peretti, *This Present Darkness* (Minstrel: Eastbourne, 1989).
[12] See Job 5:7.

Chapter Two

[1] W B Yeats, 'The Second Coming', *The Oxford Library of English Poetry*, vol III (Guild Publishing: London, 1986), p 288.

Chapter Three

[1] James 4:1–2.
[2] J R R Tolkien, *Lord of the Rings* (George Allen and Unwin: London, 1973).
[3] For a detailed consideration, see Martin Barclay, *Anxiety and Neurotic Disorders* (John Wiley and Sons: New York, 1971).
[4] Luke 15:19.
[5] See A A Hoekema, *The Christian Looks at Himself* (Eerdmans Publishing Co: Michigan, 1975).
[6] Dorothy Rowe, *Depression: The Way Out of Your Prison* (Routledge Keegan and Paul: London, 1983).
[7] R D Laing, *Self and Others* (Pelican Books: London, 1961).
[8] Daniel 5:30.
[9] For a detailed consideration, see Scott Peck, *People of the Lie* (Touchstone Books: New York, 1983).
[10] See W T Kirwan, *Biblical Concepts for Christian Counselling* (Baker Book House: Michigan, 1984), and Marjorie Foyle, *Honourably Wounded: Stress Among Christian Workers* (MARC Europe: London, 1987).
[11] John 1:5.
[12] John 12:24.
[13] Luke 9:24.
[14] Galatians 2:20.
[15] Romans 7:19.
[16] Colossians 3:9–10.
[17] Romans 8:4.
[18] Edward Sanford Martin, *My Name is Legion: Masterpieces of Religion*, ed J D Morrison (Harper and Row: New York, 1948), p 274.
[19] Peck, *op cit*, pp 73–74.
[20] Mark 5:9.
[21] Frank Peretti, *This Present Darkness* (Minstrel: Eastbourne, 1989).
[22] Matthew 6:13.
[23] John 14:16.

Chapter Four

1 Shakespeare, *Hamlet* Act III, scene 1, lines 56–60.
2 Galatians 2:11.
3 James 4:7.
4 Ephesians 6:11.
5 2 Timothy 2:22.
6 2 Corinthians 5:19.
7 Edward De Bono, *Conflicts* (Harrap: London, 1985), p 96.

Chapter Five

1 David Augsburger, *Caring Enough to Forgive* (Herald Press: Scottdale, Pennsylvania, 1981).
2 Ken and Kate Back, *Assertiveness at Work* (McGraw Hill: London, 1982), p 1.
3 Matthew 22:39.
4 Ken and Joy Gage, *Restoring Fellowship* (Moody Press: Chicago, 1984), p. 53.
5 Gavin Kennedy, *Everything is Negotiable* (Arrow Books: London, 1984), p 267.
6 Roger Fisher and William Ury, *Getting to Yes* (Hutchison Business Books: London, 1982), p 13.
7 Ephesians 2:16.
8 Colossians 1:20.
9 2 Corinthians 5:19.
10 1 Corinthians 7:11.
11 Matthew 5:24.
12 Matthew 5:23.
13 Matthew 5:24.
14 Matthew 18:15.
15 1 John 2:11.
16 *ibid.*
17 John Prebble, *Glencoe* (Penguin Books: London, 1968).
18 John 14:27.
19 J D Douglas, ed, *The New International Dictionary of the Christian Church* (Paternoster Press: Exeter, 1978), p 905.
20 2 Corinthians 5:19.
21 Romans 7:21,24.
22 Acts 2:38.
23 Luke 17:3–4.
24 Matthew 6:12.
25 David Augsburger, *Caring Enough to Not Forgive* (Herald Press: Scottdale, Pennsylvania, 1981), p 52.

[26] Proverbs 17:9.
[27] 2 Corinthians 12:20.
[28] See also William A Miller, *Make Friends with Your Shadow: How to Accept and Use Positively the Negative Side of Your Personality* (Augsburg: Minneapolis, 1981), Chapter 9.

Chapter Six

[1] Lloyd M Perry and Charles M Sell, *Speaking to Life's Problems* (Moody Press: Chicago, 1983), p 93.
[2] Luke 15:11–32.
[3] Genesis 33.
[4] Luke 15:11–32.
[5] J Grant Howard, *The Trauma of Transparency* (Multnomah Press: Portland, Oregon, 1979), p 219.
[6] David Augsburger, *Caring Enough to Not Forgive* (Herald Press: Scottdale, Pennsylvania, 1981), p 38.
[7] *ibid*, p 34.
[8] Ephesians 4:15.
[9] Luke 17:3.
[10] Theodor Seuss, *The Sneeches and Other Stories* (Random House: New York, 1961), pp 26–35.
[11] Romans 14:15.

Chapter Seven

[1] Luke 13:34.
[2] Ecclesiastes 3:8.
[3] Luke 15:11–32.
[4] Genesis 45.
[5] David Coffey, *Build That Bridge* (Kingsway: Eastbourne, 1986), p 116.

Chapter Eight

[1] K E Boulding in *Conflict Management and Problem Solving* (Frances Pinter: London, 1987), p ix.
[2] Judges 16:17.
[3] John 7:6.

Chapter Nine

[1] Clive Barrett in *Peace Together* (James Clarke and Co: Cambridge, 1987), p 128.

² Romans 5:10.
³ Exodus 2:15.
⁴ Doug McRoberts, 'The Enigma of the Man Who Fell to Earth', *The Scotsman*, 27 February 1988.
⁵ 2 Samuel 12:1–25.
⁶ Jeremiah 37:15–16.
⁷ *The Final Report: ARCIC* (SPCK/CTS, 1982), p 88
⁸ *Team Spirit* (MARC Europe: London, 1987), p 88.
⁹ Luke 10:35.
¹⁰ David Augsburger, *Caring Enough to Confront* (Herald Press: Scottdale, Pennsylvania, 1973), p 127.

Chapter Ten

¹ Scott Peck, *A Different Drum* (Simon and Schuster: New York, 1987).
² Matthew 5:9.
³ Richard E Walton, *Interpersonal Peacemaking* (Addison-Wesley Publishing Co: Reading, Massachusetts, 1969), p 71.
⁴ Olive Schreiner, quoted in *Peace Together* (James Clarke and Co: Cambridge, 1987), p 150.
⁵ Pete Meadows, *Pressure Points* (Kingsway: Eastbourne, 1988), pp 73–77.
⁶ Matthew 5:11–12.

Chapter Eleven

¹ Philippians 4:8–9.
² David C McClelland, *Power: The Inner Experience* (Irvington Publishers, Inc: New York, 1975).
³ *ibid.*
⁴ *ibid.*
⁵ Albert Ellis, *Reason and Emotion in Psychotherapy* (The Citadel Press: 1979).

Chapter Twelve

¹ Ian Mather, 'Hidden Persuaders', *The Observer Magazine* (12 July 1987): p 27.
² Esther 5:9.
³ 1 Samuel 24.
⁴ Joshua 9:16.
⁵ Judges 7:22.
⁶ Matthew 21:12.

[7] Joshua 6:15.

[8] Luke 9:10.

Chapter Thirteen

[1] Cecil Day Lewis 'Will It Be So Again?', from *Poets Queir*, ed Rintoul and Skinner (Oliver and Boyd: Edinburgh, 1976), p 411.

[2] From the last chapter of Mikhail Gorbachev, *Perestroika* (Collins: London, 1987).

INDEX

Seconds Away!

by David Cormack

Are you winning or losing? If your life is too disorganised, or too demanding, or just not going anywhere – or even going so well that you want to keep it that way – then *Seconds Away!* can help.

'This text is more than just a book,' writes Dr David Cormack. 'I have designed it as an experience for you, an experience which will equip you to live your life in a manner which gives more times of confidence, more times of satisfaction, more times of peace and rest.

Seconds Away! is a course in productive and effective living for leaders and readers of all ages and backgrounds. This could be one of the most important books you will ever buy – and one of the best investments.

'A book that can change your life – as it is changing mine.'
– Margaret Duggan, *Church Times*

David Cormack, formerly head of Training and Organisation Development at Shell International, draws upon his own extensive experience of management training and upon many other sources, particularly the Bible, for his cheerful and stimulating instruction in the art of leading a fuller, more satisfying life. He is now an international consultant to governments, businesses and charities, and Director of Cormack Consultancies. David is married with three children.

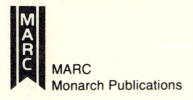

MARC
Monarch Publications

Team Spirit

by David Cormack

Whether we are leaders or followers in our offices, factories or
schools, we wishfully call our colleagues 'the team'. More often,
however, the working place is characterised by division,
disorder and dismay – anything but a team pulling and thinking
together.

In his own witty and constructive style, Dr David Cormack
tackles some of the complex issues that arise as people try to
work with others. He examines the risks and rewards of team
building, explores various styles of leadership, and discusses
delicate matters of criticism and encouragement, the use and
abuse of authority, conflict and reconciliation.

'Everyone concerned for more effective committee work and
better leadership, Christian and secular, should read *Team Spirit*
. . . Dr Cormack writes with authority and experience.'
– Church of England Newspaper

'Thorough, well researched . . . a very valuable resource tool.'
– Leadership Today

David Cormack is consultant to businesses and governments all over the
world. Formerly head of Training and Organisation Development at
Shell International, he served as Director of Management Training for
MARC Europe and now directs his own Company, Cormack
Consultancies, from the heart of Scotland.

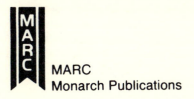

MARC
Monarch Publications